HOLD MY CROWN

WOMEN OF GRIT SHARE STORIES OF RESILIENCE

MICHELLE MRAS

Erin Baer • Charla Coleman • Amy S. Hamilton • Heather Harris
Janet Langmeier • Dapo Lipede • Susie Mosquedo • Tolu Oyewumi
Jacqueline Proffit • Colette Smith • Sally Wurr

This book is dedicated to all our tribes;
men and women who we know are
always ready to hold our crowns.

"There's three types of business
in the universe:
mine, yours and God's."

– Byron Katie

ACKNOWLEDGMENTS

I have many amazing individuals in my life who have guided me to new levels of being the best version of me… Unapologetically! Many are the authors in this book who challenged my thinking and asked me to host a writing retreat that started this entire book series.

Michael, my husband is my rock. He helps me soar, but keeps me from flying, like Icarus, too high into the sun. He guides me back home and ensures I stay healthy all while loving me to the moon and back. Your editing skills for all my books, articles and endeavors has kept me sane. I love you.

Mia and Matt, my children, are why I wrote my first two books. My life lessons were written to guide them and now, we share them around the world. My love for my babies has kept me driven.

My sisters, Yvette and Monique, have always been my supporters. My sisters are my greatest cheerleaders.

Mary (RIP) and Tony Mras for believing in me and guiding me when I felt inadequate.

David Pisarra (Mens Family Law) for helping me create a timeline and the idea for the book cover. Without your advice, this book may have been a 2022 release.

Ron and Bianca Sweeten (BRAM Consulting) are friends turned family.

Brian Swanson (Financial Services) joined me as Co-Host of the Denim and Pearls podcast during the peak of COVID-19. He and his family have welcomed me onto their porch so often, I should have my own parking spot in their driveway. I look forward to all the amazing adventures we will have as Denim and Pearls! Thank you for being a friend.

My Philippine family at The New Channel (#TNCNow), for welcoming my show Mental Shift as one of their programs.

Apple Esplana-Manansala the Co-Founder of TNCNow, for creating the Global Women Who Rule platform for so many Philippine women to shine brightly as they contribute to society.

Milko Davis (Armageddon Films) for giving me a role in his early film, Tsunambee and keeping me as a reoccurring character for sequential films. I love my time on set with the actors and crew.

Dr. Jamin Houser, Bethany and staff (Falcon Dental) for keeping my teeth healthy and strong. My smile is my calling card.

Shelly and Dallas Shepard (Harmonized Brain Centers) for helping keep my brain functioning well and my body healing from my auto accident and multiple surgical procedures.

Dr. Paul Scheele (Scheele Learning) for guiding me to discover my true self and being the voice of reason when I forget there is calm. Your Paraliminals have, and will continue to be, my saving Grace when my mind becomes unsettled.

Brother Rey Membrere and Pastor William Chancy. You both lifted me when I needed it most. I love you both.

My karaoke family who celebrate with me: Marcell (European Heels), Jennifer (INK182), Dean (Safety Station), Brian (Denim and Pearls podcast), Arlene (A2Promos) and Troy (Reichert Mortgage). I cherish the memories we create together.

Nathan (Nathan Cook Coaching) for befriending me at my first John Maxwell Team certification event. You made me laugh when I first met you and I am thrilled we have become closer throughout the years. You will always be "Bartholomew" to me.

Gary (Gary Barnes International) for believing in me and making me step out of my comfort zone to become the best version of me as a speaker coach and I cherish our friendship.

Richard Rieman (The Audiobook Wizard and Imagination Videobooks) for helping me discover my narration voice with my own book and "If I Were Your Angel". It's an honor to be on your Non-Profit Board of Directors.

Tricia Ventker (Denver Luxury Magazine and ELife Magazine) for being my support, helping me create a phenomenal media kit and for recognizing me as a Denver Woman of Influence, 2020.

Christoff J. Weihman (ASPIRE Enterprise) for creating the Ultimate Speaker Competition. I grew as a speaker by participating in this event. I met incredible people to include my publisher and friend, Ken Rochon (The Umbrella Syndicate). I'm excited for what we will create together. The future is bright with Dr. Smiley!

Jay Espitia at Culture Media Productions, his team of amazing videographers captured my story in a video business card.

Simone Sivero (Simone Vision Photography) for ensuring I am captured perfectly in all my branding photos. You make me smile like no other.

Barbara MacFerrin Photography for the beautiful photos used in many of my social media memes.

Dr Wilcox and Julie (Pikes Peak Reflux and Weight Loss) for patching me back up and saving my life. I was on a road I wasn't prepared to take. Thank you for what you do.

Jerry (RIP), Robin, Lisa and Ed. I know you will always be part of my backbone. Thank you for always knowing when to reach out to me.

Janine Bolon (The 8 Gates, Author Podcasting) you are my island sister, confidant and friend. Your Forward in this book is a gift to each Author. You are an amazing woman. I am so glad we danced into each other's lives.

TABLE OF CONTENTS

PROLOGUE

The meaning of the crown referred to in the title is based on the biblical "Crown of life" in James 1:12 and Revelation 2:10. It is bestowed upon "those who persevere under trials". This book that you hold is a compilation of stories from women I have met throughout my travels as an international speaker, communications coach, author, podcaster and internet television host.

In the Spring of 2020, a few ladies came to my cabin in the mountains of Colorado for a weekend writing retreat. Each came to enhance their ability to share their story as an inspiration to others. We quickly realized our stories shared an underlying theme which enhanced the bond amongst us. Their collective tenacity, drive and passion to share their experiences and life lessons with the world drove us to declare the necessity of creating this book.

What exactly does, "Hold My Crown" mean? Well, it is about having dignity, poise and confidence while maintaining the capability to get down to business and fight for yourself. Basically, "Hold my crown while I take care of this". We enjoyed a good laugh about the title being the dignified version of, "Hold my beer".

Do you have a preconceived notion of "normal", be it about family life, parenthood, your upbringing, or expectations as a female in society? The women in this book shared the delusion of what each thought was normal, but we instinctually knew was wrong. We each found ourselves in situations that challenged our perceptions and had to learn to trust our instincts to rise above our situations.

We learned there was no Disney ending with someone coming to save us.

We had to find our own way. Be our own hero.

"She needed a hero, so she became one."
– Unknown

We are honored you have this book in your hand. We hope that you take the time to read the stories and reach out to the author or authors that resonate with you. Remember, we share our stories to help guide others through difficult times. We each found our light at the end of the tunnel, allow us to be the light you may need in yours.

Together, we can achieve more than we can alone. Seek to be the best version of yourself every day. This collection of stories may be the guidance you were seeking to live unapologetically you.

Michelle Mras Sept 2021

CHAPTER 1
CHARLA

"Ohana is everything! We get through it together and nobody gets to quit!"

"I, Charla Coleman, live an unapologetically indomitable life! I am not defined by the trials, nor am I defeated in the trenches of my journey. I am the daughter of the Most High God and one day I will lay my crown of gems and jewels at His feet."

This is quite a strikingly bold and confident declaration, isn't it? Especially coming from a woman whose humble beginnings include being an orphaned lovechild bouncing from one foster home to another until finally being adopted at the age of six. By the time I was nine years old, I would begin running away from home to gain a sense of freedom from the normal day to day structure of house rules such as guidelines for socializing after school, mandatory house chores, bedtimes and curfew. There was also the freedom from a dark family secret (which I am not at liberty to go into full detail about in this writing since it involves a living family member. Hence, I prefer not to stir the toxic pot of family strife). However, this family secret generated deep undeserved shame and unwarranted guilt for me. This occurred at such a tender age and I would battle these demons well into my thirties which makes this secret a significant portion of my story.

I was experiencing the ramifications of my parents' sin, long before I could even understand who or what I was! These four words would echo in my mind years down the broken road of my life:

Orphaned...
Lovechild...
Dark secret...
Runaway...

This was the mantle draped over my shoulders by circumstances beyond my control and without my consent. You have now embarked on an intimate journey into the crafting of my crown.

The uncelebrated entrance I made into this world started in Hawaii when a married man had an affair with a married woman which led to my conception. Nine months later, I was born at Queens Memorial, a hospital which was lovingly serviced by nuns in those days. Within hours after delivering me, my mother left abruptly without a trace, forcing the nuns to care for me. Abandonment of newborns was a common practice in Honolulu during the 1950s through the early 1980s and was quite an epidemic in its own right. At any rate, the nuns lovingly "mothered" me for the first eight months or so of my life.

Almost a year would pass from the moment my mother left me in Queens Memorial until I would be placed in my first foster home. Somehow, my mother found out I had been inducted into the foster care system and began visiting me in the various homes I was shuffled through until an opportunity for me to be adopted surfaced, which is when I lost all contact.

Though I vaguely remember the first few years of my childhood, I do recall being described by my (adoptive) parents as shy and quiet during those days. My foster home portfolio also mentioned how I was markedly uncomfortable in the company of men. However, that was not the case when I met my soon-to-be adoptive Daddy for the first time. He and my adoptive mom had five boys and were hoping to adopt a little girl. In order to see if we would be a good fit for each other, a very relaxed meeting was arranged for my parents and I at Waikiki Beach. Shortly after being introduced to them, I began chatting with my Daddy and soon ended up on his lap! Though it would take an entire year before my adoption was all set, I had become Daddy's little girl that day we met on the beach and the judge even allowed me to go home with my forever family that day.

During the course of my new life as an adoptee, I would experience all the joys and challenges common in a typical family setting. It would take quite some time for me to adjust to routine outings, sibling rivalries, first days of school, meeting new friends, and enjoying holidays. I struggled with nestling in, but lacked the maturity to understand these challenges. The mistreatment from a family member only exacerbated the conflicts at home and would become the "dark secret" leading me to run away from home at nine years old.

Being on the run was exciting! It provided a powerful sense of freedom for me as my parents were strict and I was a habitual offender of breaking various rules. More importantly, running away became my escape from the mistreatment as well as the pressure of concealing what was going on behind closed doors, at least until I was found and returned home, time and time again. My life of running would continue intermittently until I turned 15 years old just before entering high school. By this time, I had been through a lot of therapy and the family member who was mistreating me had moved out.

Interestingly, I discovered what my name meant while taking an introductory Spanish class in high school. In Spanish, the word charla means "to have a talk, chat, give a speech." Prior to this phase of my life, the three words that described me best were withdrawn, introverted, and awkward. I remember wondering, "Why on Earth would my biological mother select such a name for me?" For the majority of my life up to that point, my personality seemed to exhibit the complete opposite of those characteristics. Aside from that, I'm not even Spanish! I am of Polynesian, Hawaiian, Maori (mother) and Nigerian (father) descent. I also wondered why she didn't give me an elegant Hawaiian name like Aolani, or Kamalei, or Lokelani. This way, I could have had more of a heritage connection with her. As it stands, I may never know the reasoning behind her choice of name for me.

By the time I entered high school, I had become socially outgoing and witty with quite a sense of humor. Without even realizing it, I had also organically developed a gift of gab. All at once, it occurred to me that my name actually fit my character and personality beautifully, just like a satin glove. This revelation felt like an unimaginable facet of freedom!

Another blessing I experienced at that time occurred while I was going to a Christian school and had accepted Christ as my Savior. This decision became a very pivotal moment in my life as so much healing washed over me the more I began delving into God's Word. I would have early morning devotions during the weekdays before classes started. This time of learning, praying, and solace in God's presence became my soul's elixir. I could feel the chains and pain of my past being lifted off of me.

I had my first serious relationship right after graduating from high school. Though my parents didn't approve of him, I dated him anyway and, eventually, moved in with him. It wasn't long after living together when his drinking and drug abuse surfaced, which led to a domestically violent lifestyle I had never been exposed to before. A pattern quickly developed. He'd get drunk and enraged then take his frustration out on me. These drunken episodes soon became frequent and extremely violent.

After sobering up, he would apologize then I would forgive him. In the next day or two, it would start all over. The shadows of this lifestyle which I hastily stepped into began to take over. Simultaneously my outgoing, witty, social butterfly type personality went on a fourteen-month hiatus. Without realizing it, I subtly grew anxious, scared, and withdrawn. Soon, I developed tremors. I learned that these symptoms are tell-tale signs of an oncoming nervous breakdown which also include depression, extreme mood swings, panic attacks, paranoia, odd happenings (flashbacks of traumatic experiences), trouble concentrating, appetite changes, and unusual sleep patterns. Looking back, I am confident I was only a few episodes away from a nervous breakdown.

On the evening of October 31, 1985, I bravely decided I was going to leave him for good at some point. As he was watching TV, I felt it was a safe moment to have the conversation letting him know our relationship had run its course. I had finally built up enough courage by the time a commercial came on and that was my cue. Positioning myself between him and the TV, I advised him of my plan to move out soon. I even agreed to let him keep everything in the apartment since I would only be taking my personal belongings. His immediate response was nothing more than a few slow nods. Foolishly, I thought that was the end of the conversation because he never took his eyes off of the TV. As I walked away from him, my initial thought was, "Wow! That went far better than I estimated!" Moments later, I had decided to go outside for some fresh air to relieve the tension I was feeling. I made it a few steps in front of the doorway when, without any warning, he bolted off the couch, ran up behind me and shoved me forward. Instinctively, I threw my hands up to catch myself from falling as I plunged into the glass panel of the screen door which shattered as my hand went straight through. As quickly as he pushed me forward, he snatched me backwards causing the back of my hand to catch onto the shards of glass that were still intact. Realizing I had sustained a wound on my hand that would obviously need medical attention, he immediately rushed me to the emergency room. However, by the time we arrived, he had formulated a lie I was to tell the hospital staff. I obliged. Two hours and twenty stitches later, we made it back home. He apologized profusely, but this time I feigned forgiveness. He fell into a deep sleep within an hour, but I was too wired up and decided I would go for the walk I had intended to earlier before the chaos.

As I began walking and contemplating, I knew I wasn't prepared financially to leave him just yet. Mentally and emotionally, I was desperate...I was done! I had come to the realization that I would have to make a swift exit when the time was right. I needed a strategy! A plan! How was I going to get away quietly and quickly? Where would I go?

As thoughts were swirling around in my head, I had walked for several blocks and needed to catch my breath. I sat down on a curb and, under the street light, I began to closely examine the mangled skin on the back of my hand that was stitched together. Feeling overwhelmed with grit and determination to get away from him, I prayed one of the simplest prayers I've ever whispered. "Lord, if anyone can get me up and out of this mess, it's You. Amen."

While still sitting on that curb and immediately after sending up that prayer, the wind began to pick up, hurling a random business card my direction which landed right in front of me! Printed on the card was an Air Force logo along with the name of a recruiter (TSgt. Terry Moore) and his phone number. I waited a few days before calling TSgt. Moore. That initial conversation with him would lead to a preliminary application, an ASVAB test, and my enrollment into the Air Force Delayed Enlistment Program. Within two weeks, I was scheduled to leave for basic training almost six months later. My boyfriend had no clue of what was brewing right under his nose. I would endure many more episodes of abuse before making it out of that hell alive.

As anticipated, I finally left him behind and started my new life of freedom in the Air Force! I spent eight weeks in Texas and four months in Mississippi before heading to my first duty station in Japan for three years. You talk about getting me up and out of my situation! Did my God deliver or did my God deliver?

After my exit from that tumultuous relationship of several near-death experiences, I would career right back down into the sinkhole of abuse three more times over the course of ten years. The worst relationship was with a man I met shortly after I joined the Air Force. We were both training for the same career field. At the time, I didn't know how to accurately describe the five years of his toxic behavior. Years later, I learned words like control freak and insecure narcissist. He was totally consumed with jealousy. This man had a list of rules for me that included how I could dress, who I could talk to, and stipulations on how I could wear perfume or makeup. He would become enraged with me if a man stood too close to me. I wasn't allowed to look a man in his eyes – he considered that flirting. I remember an incident where I was looking at a Michael Jackson album cover and he became so enraged that (in his words) I was looking at another man. We had gone fishing once and he was so insecure that when an elderly man tried to teach me how to put a worm on my hook, he flipped his lid, accusing me of flirting with the old man. I barely made it out of that abyss with my sanity. What inspired me to leave him? My two precious babies who weren't even two years old yet.

The third relationship was violent and only lasted a few months which was long enough to get pregnant with my third child.

My last relationship laced with domestic abuse was with my (ex) husband. By the time he and I met in March of 1996, I was a single-never-married mother of three young children (22 months, four and five years old). Within a month, we were married. His first assault against me came three months later on a late July evening. The police were called, pictures were taken of my injuries, and he was ordered to leave our home for 72 hours. There were no charges (I wanted him to be charged, but the police said it was my word against his, though the pictures spoke for themselves). So, he wasn't arrested and he didn't go to jail. After he left, I spent the first two nights sleeping on the floor, lodged against the door of our home terrified he was going to come back to retaliate. By the time I woke up that third morning, I was no longer terrified...I was enraged! I was furious that I had allowed myself to be reduced to sleeping on the floor of my home out of fear and that the police did absolutely nothing to hold him accountable! In that moment, I decided I would take matters into my own hands and set the proper expectation. The moment my husband returned; the tables had turned. I turned them around and introduced him to the new Charla!

My welcome home to him was a swift kick down the stairs that he was not even prepared for. I told him that's what he could expect from me going forward. For every time he even looked like he was going to strike me, every time he raised his voice to yell at me, I was going to retaliate right back. I was no longer afraid of him because I had become the aggressor. Until one day, I felt so strongly convicted by my aggressive behavior towards him that I could no longer ignore the Lord's voice that was urging me to repent. I knew it was wrong. I didn't like the aggressive abuser I had become, nor did I want my seven children to believe this is the way couples should interact. Though we didn't abuse our children, they were unavoidably impacted by our aggressive behavior. By God's grace, along with the help of so many friends, I had finally turned away from being a victim AND offender of domestic abuse by 2003.

While I am not proud of the foolish life choices I made, especially the ones which adversely impacted my children, we overcame every obstacle together by having transparent conversations about my past and my pitfalls. The greatest motivation behind my restored life is my love for my seven children, who are the absolute joys of my life!

My marriage would end in divorce after having four children together. However, our irreconcilable differences were completely unrelated to the domestic violence we had overcome.

Through every phase of motherhood, I put great effort into teaching my children all of the life lessons that would make them wise, Godly, successful, and safe. When I became a single Mom in 2005, my commitment to teach them well only grew stronger as I never wanted any of my children to go through the hell I had endured, especially when I was a young adult. I made up quotes to reiterate the importance of family and one of my favorite quotes is, "Ohana is everything! We get through it together and nobody gets to quit!"

That quote has become a verbal banner that my children and I hold onto especially after our worst nightmare came to pass two years ago.

In early December of 2018, my youngest daughter entered her first serious relationship with a 22-year-old man she met online. Within three weeks, they moved in together and got engaged. Soon, Jackie started sharing interactions and behaviors that were very similar to those of my narcissistic boyfriend. I encouraged her to end the relationship multiple times, but she felt she was in too deep. However, just four months into their relationship, Jackie had texted me to say she was sorry she didn't listen to me and that she knew she was going to leave him soon. Despite my reassurance that she wasn't in too deep, she just wasn't ready.

On May 14, 2019, Jackie and her fiancé had gotten into an argument while she was on the phone with my oldest son. When my son notified me, we called her together with intentions of getting her out of there. Tragically, her fiancé shot and killed her while she was on the phone with us before he turned the gun on himself.

Jackie was the kindest, gentlest human I've ever had the privilege of spending almost 19 short years with. She was angelic with the softest touch and had the sweetest disposition in the world.

After she was ripped away from us, I began doubting if I was even equipped well enough to influence my own children to recognize the red flags of a toxic individual or relationship. Then suddenly, by the grace of God, I remembered her words of apology for not listening to me when I tried to warn her. That moment of revelation fueled me – in the midst of doubt and grief – with all the reassurance I needed. Indeed, I AM equipped and I DO have the influence to prevent other young women like Jackie from falling prey to narcissistic, toxic, domestically abusive relationships!

In May 2021, I launched my organization, Jackie's W.A.R. (Women At Risk). I am on a lifelong mission to prevent this tragedy from happening to any other woman because prevention is the key to eradicating domestic abuse. Death doesn't get to rip my daughter away from me and think I'm just going to quietly fade off into the sunset of life! That will never be my response or my story!

God has prepared me – Charla – to boldly speak out about Jackie's tragedy. I will not sit back silent, withdrawn, or timid.

This is my calling: To travel around the globe embracing, empowering, and educating women to be proactive in respecting themselves in their relationships unapologetically. I will forever speak out against domestic abuse. Every time I share Jackie's story, another jewel is added to my crown. So, go ahead...... hold my crown. I've got work to do!

Charla Coleman enjoyed a military career in Intelligence and Morse Code Operations for the United States Air Force before finding her passion to serve the community through various non-profits. She was employed for eight years with Compassion International in the Sponsor Donor Relations and Trips & Visits departments. Charla is currently a Board Member for Lupus Colorado, the Toastmasters VP of Membership for Rocky Mountain Toastmasters Club 739 and volunteers for Mary's Home. After tragically losing her teenage daughter to domestic violence in 2019, Charla created an organization in May 2021, Jackie's W.A.R. (Women at Risk). It is dedicated to preventing girls and women from falling into the snare of domestic abuse. Charla also collaborates with local advocates and agencies to rescue women in domestic crisis.

A native of Hawaii, now settled in Colorado Springs, Charla is a proud mother of seven children and a cat. When she isn't working at Mary's Home, she can be found enjoying time with family, friends, or exploring the beautiful outdoors.

Chapter 2
AMY

A woman who is passionate about project management, public speaking and shoes.

I don't remember the first time my dad hit me, and I can't specifically remember the last time. I do, however, clearly remember the worst time he hit me. This is not something that I have shared with many people, but after almost fifty years on this amazing planet and living a fabulous life, I feel that it is a story that may help and perhaps inspire others.

I have often glossed over or embellished my childhood, as a young adult I wanted to be accepted and growing up poor white trash, is not something that you discuss in polite social circles. My experience as a teenager helped me to get through one of my toughest struggles as a professional in the workplace. When faced with a bully who was mentally and emotionally abusing our staff, I relied upon the tough foundation my life was built on to do the right thing in a tough situation. We all have a story to share on overcoming adversity and obstacles. I hope mine will reach a few hearts that need to hear it.

Let me provide you with a little background about my parents. My parents met in junior high school and they were married until my father passed away several years ago of a massive heart attack. My mother planned her wedding as a project for her home economics class her senior year of high school and their wedding was a few weeks after she graduated, the year was 1969. My Dad was a high school dropout working at a grocery store as a bagger. My older sister was born nine months to the day from their wedding – trust me, as soon as we found out about the birds and the bees, we did the math. I was born a year and half after my sister. My brother was born almost two years after me, making him the baby and the only boy.

My parents were woefully unprepared to have three young children always hungry, continuously outgrowing clothes, and constantly demanding new things. As I grew up, I took an interest in the bills and household finances, by the fourth grade, I was managing our weekly grocery list based on the local store specials. I began calculating our monthly budget based on household income, there were no college or retirement savings plans, we were always on the edge. My parents were savvy enough to buy a house from a government program and we were always on the precipice of losing the house because of late payments or the property taxes being in arrears.

Throughout elementary school, my father had been in and out of multiple jobs and eventually completed his GED. My mother worked as a crossing guard for the city while we were in elementary school but started working full time as an administrative assistant when I was in junior high. I started managing a schedule for after school television watching for my siblings and a household chore schedule. If my siblings did not follow my schedules I would report them to my mother and deduct their meager allowances – I managed the finances after all.

As a teenager, I was becoming more competent. I was also becoming more arrogant. I began delivering papers for my first paper route when I was eleven, added some sporadic babysitting jobs at twelve, and by the time I was fourteen, I had a work permit and spent one glorious summer working at the local public library. I maintained an A/B average in school and did my best to stay out of teenage drama. At the same time, I grew to respect my parents less, especially my father. I viewed him as not being a provider for the family and the reason why my mother had to work. The more I viewed myself as an adult, the less I felt like I had to listen to my father. Meanwhile, my mother indulged me because I was managing most of the household responsibilities.

It was during this time when my father was struggling and periodically was laid off from work that he would sometimes take out his frustration on me physically. There was a fairly regular cycle of my ignoring him and not speaking to him, followed by a screaming match, cumulating in a backhand or two to the face. This was something that my siblings and I decided to keep quiet about and not tell my mother. We also knew better than to tell any other adult as we had friends in the foster care system and being hit a few times seemed a lot better than stories we heard about that system. Any visible injury was easily explained away by my own natural clumsiness and attributed to rough play and sports.

When these episodes occurred, my dad would boast that when he was my age that his dad would "knock him across the room into a wall and he wouldn't even cry." He would regale me with stories of how he was whipped with an electrical cord when he was a boy. He would tell me that it was "for my own good" and that "I was too big for my britches." I would yell back and tell him that I was going to go to college and make something of myself. I would scream back, "I am not going to be like you. I am going to be successful. "

Reflecting upon it later, I realized that he was trying to teach me the only way that he knew how. By hitting me, he was trying to put me into what he perceived as my place. My father was the fifth of eight children and college had not been a priority for his family. My mother was the fifth of six children and only one of her siblings had been to college. I believe now, that in his mind, it was better for me to be knocked down by him, than for me to be knocked down by the world. He didn't believe there was a path for me to go to college and my words were hurtful and spiteful.

I did not understand these things at the time and my defiance and resentment continued to grow. One time when I was carrying a basket of laundry and I needed to pass him in a narrow hallway, we were in one of our silent non-speaking phases of the cycle, neither of us moved. I glared at him and waited for him to move out of my way. Without the normal yelling and screaming, he stepped forward and backhanded me hard into a wall. Perhaps I should have realized that things were escalating, but hindsight is much easier than foresight.

Despite the most significant beating that occurred between us, I continued to live at home. At sixteen, I started my senior year of high school and there were a few more altercations with my father. This eventually led to him kicking me out of my childhood home. I too was very stressed as I was in an advanced program for high school and had a part time job carrying about thirty hours a week. I was in a program that only required me to attend high school part time and was attending community college classes to get a head start on college. For the first few weeks, I rotated between some of my friends' houses. Eventually it was worked out that I could stay with my maternal grandfather for the rest of the school year.

I started college at Eastern Michigan University as a naive girl from a small town. I quickly learned that life was easier if you did not mention a harsh upbringing or financial challenges. I had always known that I would have to pay for my tuition and had to balance, work, school, and being in the Michigan Army National Guard. When I went through Basic Training, I thought drill sergeants were annoying, not intimidating. They certainly could not compare to the level of rage that my father used to shout at me, and they weren't allowed to hit you. Other young women told me that this was the worst experience of their lives. I wished that I could say the same.

In the Army, academia, and my civilian career I thrived and enjoyed my life. I met my husband in Kosovo and traveled throughout Europe and the Middle East. By my forties, my life had become so amazing that I had to start creating new dreams. I lived a life beyond what I ever imaged in my childhood. I had a great job, wonderful friends, and a cabin in the Rocky Mountains. I really had everything I could imagine.

Despite not liking his job and no longer having any chance of being promoted in his military career, my husband wanted to move back to Germany. He wanted to go alone and for me to stay behind and watch our house and cabin. We had spent years barely seeing each other due to both of our jobs and his military deployments. I couldn't believe that he wouldn't retire and instead wanted to leave for a three-year tour in Germany without me.

The day before he was scheduled to leave for Germany, I shattered the bone in my left foot and found out I would have to have surgery to fix it. He still got on the plane. I was fortunate to have some terrific girlfriends who supported me through the entire experience. My bone was repaired with a plate and five screws, but my marriage was not so easily fixed. While I was on crutches for six months, I also separated from my husband of over a decade. After trying to work it out long distance, I decided that the only way to try to repair our fractured marriage was to move to Germany.

When I interviewed with my future boss, I was super excited and looking forward to the next phase of my life. It was difficult to put my house in the city on the market, but at least I had friends who would be the caretakers of our remote cabin while I was away. When I arrived at the airport in Germany, my husband picked me up and I had every hope that we could rebuild. I was looking forward to my new position and excited about the future.

I had taken on the role of the deputy, so the only person in my organization above me was my boss. There were three supervisors, all military that worked directly for my boss. When I first met one of the supervisors, I told him I was excited to be there and had a fantastic interview with the boss. He gave me an odd look and I felt my first sense of foreboding. He was careful and measured in what he said to me and I felt that there were many things being left unsaid.

After just a few days in Germany, I felt like I made an enormous mistake. My new boss hadn't even given me time to find a house and was making demands that I start taking care of business at work. I didn't even have a car to get to work and had to pay for a rental car. He began calling me and demanding that I check my blackberry day and night. I was so busy in my new job that I didn't have time to think about working on my failing marriage.

My site at work was remote and my staff were desperately unhappy. When I first began asking questions of them, they would either be hostile toward me or fearful. When I approached them about projects, they were resentful, scared, and nervous. I felt a constant tension and was unsure of the best way to proceed. This was a staff of highly trained career professionals, comprised of active duty, civilians, and contractors, I was baffled by their behavior. I had been working for the Department of Defense in one capacity or another for over twenty-five years and couldn't fathom why my staff were behaving so oddly.

I spoke to a few of my professional colleagues about the situation and that is when I started finding out the rumors about my boss. I was told that he was known for being a slave driver and only cared about results, not his team. He was well known in the community as one that you had to be careful working with because he had a reputation for not always being ethical. My old colleagues warned me to be careful and that my boss was known to be very vengeful if he felt he was crossed.

I eventually met and spoke with the person who had the position before me, and his story made me immediately regret my decision to work under this man as his second in charge. He told me that my boss used to demand that he call staff while they were at the airport to not go on vacation for frivolous reasons. He said that my boss constantly pitted the staff against each other and was always trying to keep everyone on edge. He reported that the boss had asked him to compromise his integrity and ethics on numerous occasions and the few times he did compromise due to fear of retribution and losing his job. He told me that he was offered a promotion to stay in the organization and the boss said, "If you take this position, I will own you."

I felt a sense of strain at work that I had never experienced before in my professional life. The main organization was located on a base just a few miles away, but it felt like hundreds. My boss spent half the day there. Those people saw the person that I had when I interviewed with him just a short time before. At our remote base he was the highest-ranking person and the big bully on campus. My boss would strut around the office when he came in and constantly remind everyone how important he was.

In the mornings while he was gone the staff began to cheer up a bit and some started to confide more in me. I started to implement some small programs to try to improve morals, like a potluck breakfast once a month. When my boss noticed that the staff were starting to come to me, his deputy, he wasn't happy. He would make small comments to undermine me in front of the staff, instead of supporting my efforts. When the staff heard my boss come into the office, they would visibly shutdown and try not to draw attention to themselves.

I began to hear more stories from the staff about my boss that had me concerned about possible illegal activities which may have taken place prior to my arriving in the organization. They told me that equipment had been given away without proper authorities. My team confided in me that contract negotiations may not have been handled in an ethical manner. I was told that there had been late night parties, fraternization, and possibly sexual assault.

I was overwhelmed and disheartened. I didn't have my network of close friends nearby like I had when I broke my foot. My marriage was hanging on by a thread and despite having moved halfway across the world, I barely had time to see my husband. At work, I was torn on what to do and the best way to approach the situation. When I tried to talk to my boss, he would mock the situation and tell me that I had no reason for concern. When I questioned him on some budget issues, he removed me and put a very junior person on the project.

I sought out the counsel of one of the human resources professionals and told them about the situation in my office. I informed them that I could not prove any of the stories I had heard, but that I believed my staff were telling me the truth. Especially as there were so many stories from multiple people. She told me that as a new person I wasn't responsible, but that if I stayed in the organization, I would be. She told me that by not taking action I was complicit to the behavior actions of the boss. Also, that the longer I was in the organization, I would move from being complicit, to being culpable for his actions.

The situation weighed heavily on me: I started having problems sleeping at night. I constantly felt the strain of work. Not the job itself, but the irrational demands of a tyrannical boss. He would send information to one member of the leadership team and ask them to send it to another late at night, just to ensure we were all checking our emails. I started thinking about how I could transfer jobs to another organization. I started to call friends in my network. I knew I needed out of that toxic environment.

My boss began to try to intimidate me.

He would get awfully close to me physically. One time even pulling up his chair directly in front of me and tapping on my notepad that was sitting in my lap. I was wearing a skirt. I felt very vulnerable and I could feel his breath on my neck as his hand was dangerously close to the hem of my skirt. One of my peers who witnessed this asked me about it afterwards. He thought it was inappropriate behavior and told me that if a man did that to his wife, he would react with physical violence.

My boss had no barriers and no boundaries. His wife was a sweet woman who adored him despite his flaws. She once told me when she was looking for him that she knew that if anything ever happened to her that he wouldn't be found, and she would die alone. She would bring homemade food to the office for the team. After she left the office, he would loudly proclaim, "My fat, ugly, Mexican wife dropped off food" and "She may not be much to look at but that Mexican bitch can cook." My staff would come to me and tell me that the statements my boss made about his wife offended them. When I approached my boss about the issue he became irrationally upset and told me he could call his wife anything he wanted and it was none of my business.

My boss told me that one of the other senior staff members had an anger management problem and had been referred to the clinic for counseling. My teammate was on active duty and admitted that he was suffering from a serious case of PTSD. He told me that he was lucky his wife was being supportive of him through his time of need. One day my boss came to my office and said, "Watch this." He then proceeded to go to my teammates office and deliberately provoke him. My boss taunted him until my teammate lost control, turning red in the face and yelling. I stood by silently watching, unsure of how to deescalate the situation. Afterwards my boss stopped by my office and said, "See, I can spin him up whenever I want." I felt sick to my stomach.

My other teammate was terrified of the boss. He told me several stories about the boss's unethical and immoral behavior. I asked him why he didn't do anything to stop it. He told me that my boss had the ability to destroy his military career and that he had been threatened several times. He told me that he was afraid that if he did bring it up to the headquarters that they wouldn't listen and there would be reprisals.

One of the younger team members on the staff came in late one day. When I asked him where he had been, he responded, "Why? Did you think I hanged myself?" I asked him to come by my office. I asked him if he had been thinking of suicide. He responded, "Not really, mostly I just daydream that I get in a car accident and go into a coma until this tour is over." A few days later he made another joke after a sports injury to his head. He said, "Too bad I wasn't hit harder, because at least if I died, I wouldn't have to work here anymore. This was the same junior member who my boss had assigned the budget. This junior member was genuinely concerned that he wasn't trained. My boss wanted him to sign off for contracts worth significant amounts of money. He was also working long hours and his wife was very unhappy with the situation.

Another one of my team members started to talk about drinking all the time. He said the only way he could cope with the job was to go home and drink a bottle of whisky a night. When I asked him if he was serious, he didn't hesitate in responding yes. He told me that he couldn't imagine working someplace like this in his military career and that if he had an option, he would quit. He said that our boss made him ashamed to be in the military.

The military members had no option, but to stay in the organization. The civilians on the other hand did. The turnover rate was excessively high. When compared to our sister organization just ten miles away, the numbers were staggering. We had a 200% higher turnover rate. Civilians often asked for curtailments or found new jobs in the local area. Contractors asked to be assigned to new organizations or quit if they couldn't get a position within their company. The high turnover in the organization created confusion which was something that my boss was able to exploit. When I brought up the retention issue to him with a spreadsheet, he lashed out at me verbally. He accused me of trying to create problems, defying the logic that I had only been with the organization a few months and he had been there for almost two years. I kept thinking that if someone harmed themselves in this situation, I was partly responsible. Part of me knew that if I continued to leverage my network I could get out of that toxic environment. My survival instinct is strong. I wanted to flee from the verbal abuse and mind games. Even though I could have left, I knew that I had to stay to help. I reflected to when I was a teenager and the worst time my father had ever hit me.

I hadn't thought about the negative aspects of my childhood in years, but under these circumstances, I used it to give me strength. The situation at work was so bad that for the first time as an adult, I felt helpless. Some people may think that mental and emotional abuse is not as bad as physical abuse, but after experiencing both, I feel that mental and emotional abuse can be far more damaging.

Unable to sleep and feeling that I couldn't abandon the people working for this cruel toxic man, I thought about the darkest point of my life up until then. When I was a teenager, my father had been angry that the dishes weren't done. I informed him which of my siblings were responsible according to the chores chart and considered the matter settled. He didn't see it that way and informed me that I needed to do the dishes. I told him that I didn't have to listen to him, which earned me a sharp backhand across the cheek.

Normally that would have been the end of it, but in this case, I didn't cower and remain quiet. I stood up to my father and told him I didn't care how many times he hit me. He struck me again, this time harder along the jaw. I bit my tongue. I could feel the metal taste of blood in my mouth. "Hit me again," I yelled at him. He struck me a third time along the temple and ears, I could feel them ringing and felt slightly dizzy.

I was beyond the pain, I no longer cared. The next blow was a backhand across my face with his forearm. I was knocked backward into our dining room table and slumped to the floor. Everything below my waist was numb. "I don't care if you kill me," I shrieked at my father. The blows were raining down on my head. I feebly tried to protect my face. I could feel the swelling and my words were slurring. The world around me was becoming a hazy shade of red. Still, I taunted my father with my words. I genuinely believed that the hitting would never cease. When people use the phrase, "a world of hurt", this was my world in that moment.

I was surprised when the blows paused for a moment. I tried to see what was distracting my father through my blackening eyes, dripping with mingled tears and blood. I could make out my younger brother. He was on my dad's back. With the ringing in my ears, my brother's words were not clear, but he was yelling at him to stop hitting me. My father stopped hitting me only because he was now trying to hit my brother. My brother yelled at me, "Run!"

I couldn't feel my toes. Everything below my waist, from where I hit my back on the dining room table, was numb. My brother continued to yell for me to run, while nimbly dodging the blows from my father. Taunting him to follow as he made his way to the front door and the safety outside. It seemed like I was getting up in slow motion. I had to roll onto my stomach and push myself up from the floor. I stumbled through the house to the back door, barefoot, I made my way to a friend's house. Her mom was a nurse and wanted to take me to the hospital, but I begged her not to take me or report it.

Now, all these year later, I let myself relive the pain of that experience. I didn't focus on the part that I had experienced, but on my brother's bravery. My brother was younger and smaller than me. There would have been no blame if he went to his room and hid, but he didn't. He stood up to a bully who was much large than him. He faced the challenge and didn't just think about only saving himself, he saved me.

I thought about the people who worked for me and I knew that I couldn't abandon them to the monster that was abusing them.

I needed to be strong and stand up to the bully the same way my brother had stood up to my father all those years ago. When you have the ability to help people being abused you have a responsibility to do so and not turn your back to those in need. I knew that despite wanting to save myself. I had a responsibility to pay it forward. Someone had risked themselves to save me and now I had the opportunity to do the same.

The next day, with a grave amount of fear of retribution, I asked to speak to the second highest leader in the organization. I reported my concerns of the illegal, immoral, and unethical leadership impacting my team and requested an investigation. I could see the skepticism in his eyes. Despite what I had personally seen and the stories from the staff, I could tell he didn't believe me. When I specifically reported my concern that someone may commit harm to themselves to include suicide, his attitude changed. The military has an extremely high rate of suicide. The command would be investigated with a high level of scrutiny and reflect very adversely on the organization. It was only then that I finally had his attention. He stopped treating me like a weak woman and agreed to "look into" the situation. After a discussion with the team member who I thought may be suicidal, a formal investigation was launched.

From that day until the findings of the investigation, my life was a living hell. My boss who had been toxic before vacillated between trying to be charming and reverting to his true nature. It wasn't until years later that I would hear the term "gas-lighting". Now I know that was a signature move for my old boss. He would tell one story one day and the next say that he never said it. He created misinformation among the staff and doled out guidance and information sparingly. I often felt like I was crazy.

I wondered if somehow after so many years of being a performer that I had fallen down a rabbit hole.

A few days after I made the allegations against him, he pulled me into his office to chat. He said he had been hearing rumors and asked if he should be concerned. I replied that if his actions were legal, ethical, and moral that he shouldn't have anything to worry about.

The work itself wasn't bad, but the environment was stifling. The boss was constantly shifting work around and creating chaos. It was as if every day I was living out the chapters of The Prince by Machiavelli. There was a sense of urgency that we had to meet the boss needs no matter what. My boss began to pull staff members into his office individually. They would come out disheartened and shaken. Several informed me that he threatened their careers if he found out that they said anything against him.

He pulled me into his office and made comments about how it was difficult to fire career government officials after they had passed their probationary period. He told me that even if he gave me a bad evaluation, I would just go on a performance plan. I told him that I was aware and if he had a problem with my work performance, I needed to know what it was so that it could be corrected. He had nothing specific, but I could tell he was devising a new plan. He told me stories of how he had driven people to quit in his old organizations.

I had another long sleepless night about work. I barely had time to think of my personal life. Even when I saw my husband on weekends, I was constantly taking phone calls and answering emails. My husband was increasingly upset with me. He stated that I didn't want to work on our marriage and always put my career first. I had left a great job, a wonderful network of friends, and a city I loved to try to save my marriage. Instead, I had a job that was crushing my spirit, most of my closest friends were several time zones away, and I was completely failing at saving my marriage.

When the investigator arrived from the United States, the office reached a crescendo of tension. Several staff members came into my office and asked what they should say, often stating that they feared for their jobs. I always responded with a question, "What are your core values?" In the military members are taught core values that vary slightly by service. These core values include traits like duty, honor, integrity, respect, and selfless service. I would remind each person that they had core values to live up to. As long as they told the truth to the investigator, they were living up to their core values. I reminded them that we all had a duty to do what was legal, moral, and ethical every day. No one was exempt.

Despite the strength I displayed at work and to my team, I was terrified. For the first time, instead of being viewed as a honest and respected professional, I was being treated as a pariah. The leadership at the headquarters appeared to believe that I was making up the allegations and "to protect me" they transferred me under a new supervisor. I was given a written counseling statement for the first time in my life. I continued to network and even though I was working on an opportunity to leave, I knew I couldn't until I had ensured justice was done for the team. Abandoning them was not an option.

I began to stress eat, my sleep quality was poor, I didn't have time to work out, and I began putting on weight. My husband made it clear when he saw me that the decline in my physical appearance wasn't helping to resolve our marital problems. The constant work calls and doing work on weekends was adding to the stress. I felt lonely, like I had no support. One of my few friends told me I looked sick and was worried for my health. I knew that I had to keep it together and be strong.

Every day I went into the office with my hair coiffed, my makeup on, and presented a smile to the world while on the inside I felt like my light was fading. The tension at work increased when the investigator left. We still didn't know the results. I felt knots in my stomach and hoped that the results would be presented quickly. The waiting was the hardest part. I kept telling my team to have hope, while inside I was terrified that we would all receive major repercussions for our actions.

Finally, the results of the investigation were announced. My boss was removed from the organization. There were 28 affidavits filed against him with incidents over two years. After the results were reported my acting supervisor gave me a begrudging apology and stated that he had thought I was just a troublemaker. He said that he hadn't realized that things were so bad and that it was the fault of those in the organization for not reporting it. I told him that was a "blaming the victim" mentality. Despite the investigation resulting in the removal of my boss, some people looked for excuses to exonerate his behavior.

Immediately following the investigation, I realized that I was woefully unprepared to deal with the hurt and pain that my staff was finally able to express. I read an article about how people dealt with toxic environments by either flight, fight, or freeze. Those that had been able to leave had exercised the option to flee. Now I was left with those who were angry and still had fight, like my teammate with the PTSD or those that no longer had any energy, those that were frozen from fear.

I realized that rebuilding the organization would be much harder than I imagined. Everyone on the team was very damaged. Some members who had been too afraid to talk when my old boss was there confided their stories to me. I didn't feel like any of my leadership training had prepared me for dealing with the aftermath of this type of situation. I had a friend who had recently taken over an organization after the boss had been relieved. We shared antecedents about what worked and what wasn't working. I had volunteered at a domestic violence shelter and done some training with them in the past. I started treating my staff with the same techniques I learned from that meager training. Mostly, I just listened to their heartbreaking stories. I tried to give them hope that everything would eventually be okay. My colleague and I both discussed that you can find a lot of articles about toxic leadership and organizations, but very little on how to help an organization recover from toxic leadership.

After a few months of assisting the organization's recovery, I moved on to a new job a few miles away with a bright future and people I knew. I once again felt valued and appreciated at work. I was able to arrange my schedule to go to the gym and stopped stress eating. I made an honest attempt at that point to work things out with my husband, but unfortunately, it couldn't be salvaged. The details I will perhaps share in another story.

The tales of triumph and heartbreak from my old team never ceases to overwhelm me. One young team member met me for coffee with his wife and toddler. They informed me that her bags were packed and she was planning to leave the day that the investigation started. They told me that my courage to stand up to our old boss had saved their marriage.

The team member that I had worried might harm himself is excelling in his career. His wife and children are doing well and they still remember the Christmas party I had at my house shortly after our old boss was gone. As coincidence would have it, we discovered that I used to serve with his oldest brother when I was on active duty. His brother told him that if anyone could fix it, I could. He told me that a year later people could hardly imagine the old organizational climate. He tells them that I was a guardian angel sent to help them during their darkest hour.

There were twelve follow-on investigations from my time working for my old boss, one for each month that I worked there. Some involved missing equipment, others involved questionable contract practices. The worst involved a DUI and the end of the career for one of the members of the team. The member that had been struggling with alcohol abuse under my old boss succumbed to his addiction. I was asked to serve as a character witness of the extenuating circumstances of our old organization. Though not an expert in the area, I witnessed that when people are asked to constantly compromise their core values, it eats away at their soul. I passionately believe that my team member coped with the compromises he made to his core values by drinking the pain away. Sometimes, I wonder if I could have done more to help prevent him from imploding, destroying his career, since the risk he took could have resulted in killing another.

I still stay in touch with many members of the team and they stay in touch with each other. We have a shared bond of going through deep emotional and mental trauma together. When we talk about that time it is with hushed voices and a sense of disbelief. When you read the stories of abusive and toxic environments you think that people exaggerate. When I talk to my old team members, we all know that it was real and we each carry scares.

Many underestimate emotional and mental abuse, but I believe it can have the worst and most lasting impact. I have been physically beaten as a child and I was in the Green Zone in Iraq. Yet the time I worked for this man was the worst experience of my life. I am grateful that my tough childhood prepared me for the challenge. I am grateful for my friends and family who, though hours away, took my calls and bolstered me on the darkest of days when I felt that the burden was too great to bear.

Two years later I presented at TEDxStuttgart on "The Secret to Life from a PMP" and the next year I published my first book "Life is a Project." I started a PhD program in organizational leadership and am working on my dissertation. I left Stuttgart Germany to work for the Executive Office of the President of the United States. Recently I published my second book "The Consummate Communicator: Character Traits of True Professionals" and started a monthly Livecast "24 Authors in 12 Hours." Most importantly, I have an amazing network of friends and family that surround me with love.

What my father never realized is that instead of beating the arrogance out of me, he beat the confidence into me. Laying on that dining room floor wondering when the next blow would reign down upon my face taught me that I am strong. My brother showed me that even if you are weaker and smaller, you can still protect those that you care about. Throughout my life, I have not only survived, but I have also thrived.

Amy S. Hamilton is a project manager, author, motivational speaker, and shoe aficionado. She presented on the "The Secret to Life from a PMP" at TEDxStuttgart in September 2016. She is an award-winning public speaker and has presented in over twenty countries on overcoming adversity, reaching your dreams, computer security and project management. She served in the Michigan Army National Guard as a communications specialist and was commissioned into the US Army Officer Signal Corp, serving on Active Duty and later the US Army Reserves. She has worked at both the US European Command and the US Northern Command & North American Aerospace Defense Command (NORAD) on multiple communications and IT projects.

Amy holds a Bachelor of Science (BS) in Geography, from Eastern Michigan University, a Master of Science (MS) in Urban Studies from Georgia State University, Master in Computer Science (MSc) from the University of Liverpool, Master Certificate in Project Management (PM) and Chief Information Officer (CIO) from the National Defense University, and completed the US Air University, Air War College. She is currently a doctoral candidate at Regent University in their Organizational Leadership Doctorate of Philosophy (PhD) Program.

CHAPTER 3
COLETTE

"Forgive, overcome and learn to love again."

If you really think about it, surviving all that childhood brings can be a miracle. My childhood was not very different from anyone else's. This was what I thought when I was young; everyone else had the same childhood I did.

Most of us have a few vivid memories from our childhood. Some stand out more than others; but if you are like me, there isn't much other than quick snapshots of memory like a slide show, bits and pieces. From these bits and pieces, our lives are defined as well as those around us. This is true for all of us but for me it is especially true because of my childhood.

It is 1973. I am six years old. My younger siblings, David and Carolyn and I are playing in the living room. The couch is a light yellow with a paisley print, a little worn but well loved. The sun is shining through the large picture window as we play with our toys on the old wide planked wooden floor. The smell of eggs and toast wafts out of the kitchen and my tummy starts to rumble reminding me that I am hungry. Suddenly, there is yelling coming from the kitchen. "Leave me alone, Woman! You're stupid! Don't make me teach you a lesson!" My mom is begging and pleading with my dad but it isn't helping. I sneak up to the kitchen doorway and peek in around the corner. My whole body is shaking. I am scared because I have experienced this before. I look over my shoulder at my siblings and beg with my eyes for them to be quiet.

Shhhhh!

When I glance back through the kitchen doorway, Daddy suddenly grabs Mommy by her hair and starts banging her head into the old green Formica counter top. Loud banging sounds can be heard throughout the small house. My brother and sister start crying.

Shhhhh!

As my mom's head continues to bang off the counter top, she makes eye contact with me and screams, "RUN!!"

I RUN!

This is one of the first vivid memories of my childhood. Some memories were better. My dad, Michael Lionel Levesque, was an alcoholic. My parents met when they were teenagers in Squamish, British Columbia. Squamish is a picturesque little town located at the north end of Howe Sound.

My dad was in and out of my life during my childhood due to his alcohol and drug issues. My Mom, Karen, did her best to survive, protect her children and hold things together so that we were okay. She is one of the strongest and bravest women I know. Looking back, I think she coped by controlling things within her power because everything around us felt so out of control. I know for certain she wanted a better life for her kids. To this day, I need control, routine and order so that I can manage the daily details of life. Otherwise, life feels uncomfortably messy.

Like any family, we had good days and bad days.

One of my favorite childhood memories was when I was seven. Anytime Daddy returned home it was what I like to call "the honeymoon phase". I remember he helped us build a fort out of pillows and blankets in the living room. You know, the kind where multiple blankets are thrown over the backs of furniture and inside it is loaded with more blankets and lots of pillows not to mention toys. Lots of toys! We spent the whole afternoon playing in that fort. Daddy brought out his guitar and we sang some of our favorite songs. My particular favorite was Wolverton Mountain by Claude King. Imagine three tiny children dancing around the living room while singing at the top of their lungs.

"They say don't go on Wolverton Mountain
If you're looking for a wife
'Cause Clifton Clowers has a pretty young daughter
He's mighty handy with a gun and a knife."

We begged to sleep in the fort that night. To my joy, our wish was granted! I remember being amazed that we didn't have to sleep in our beds. We snuggled in the fort with music in our heads and joy in our hearts. In the morning, we woke up early and we found Daddy was already up and in the bathroom shaving. As we looked and gaped at his reflection in the bathroom mirror, I saw that his whole face was covered in shaving cream. He looked funny with all that white goop on his face. The three of us snuck up behind him and yelled "MAD DOG MAD DOG!! "Daddy chased us around the living room, in and out of the fort, growling and snarling while we screamed and giggled in joy. That game lasted for a good hour. We often begged to play Mad Dog. It was silly, rambunctious and a lot of fun.

Though my childhood had many good times, as I look back through my memories, they are mostly filled with memories of my dad being in and out of my life. When he was in my life, it almost never ended well. When he came back into our lives after a long absence, it was always with gifts, joy and hope that this time it would last. It NEVER lasted.

There were times when Mum would take Daddy back because he was clean and sober. Daddy came back again and he has a job, so we are all happy! Though I am young, I know this won't last long. I'm barely eight when Daddy relapses. This time he wasn't just drinking but he was also using drugs. I don't remember all the details. I just remember it was bad. Mum tells Daddy, "If you come home drunk again, I will meet you at the top of the stairs and throw you out for good. I've had enough!" One night, I was in a deep sleep, snuggled in my bed. Loud noises interrupted my dreams. Yelling drew me out of my bed. Daddy was yelling again. He didn't sound right. His speech was slurred and he was really angry. I peeked around the corner. My Mum had a huge green duffle bag and stood at the top of the stairs. She looked so determined. She yelled at my dad, "Get out NOW!" She threw that huge duffle bag down the stairs at him. I snuck back to bed and hid under my covers for the rest of the night. I felt scared and alone. I wanted to be invisible! Daddy was gone once again. This time for good.

By the time I was eight, my parents weren't together anymore. Mum still made an effort to make sure I could spend time with Daddy when he was sober. One Summer, she agreed that I could go to a farm with Daddy and Uncle Phil to pick berries for a good portion of summer break. I was so excited because it meant time with my Daddy. Imagine a huge berry farm with acres of berries and several wooden bunk houses each with rows of bunk-beds for seasonal workers. Rows and rows of fresh, sweet, red strawberries waited to be picked and eaten. At first, it was great. I enjoyed haphazardly picking berries during the day and relaxing around the fire in the evening. There were other kids there so playing and having fun was a full-time job.

Then the evening parties, drinking and fighting started. Dad kept getting into scuffles with the other seasonal workers. Finally, Dad and I were moved into our own small bunkhouse, but Dad was never there. I got sick with a cold and severe laryngitis but Dad still wasn't there. The farmer's daughter took care of me for the few days I was sick which felt strange to me. I woke up one morning and Daddy passed out on the floor. I couldn't get Daddy up but I wanted to go home. I knew I had to go home! I couldn't find my uncle and I couldn't wake him up. When he finally got up hours later, I demanded to go home. He wanted to stay and told me to hitchhike home. I was so scared I would never get home and no one would know what happened to me. He finally agreed we needed to leave so we hitchhiked to the closest bus stop and made our way home. I asked a lot of questions, "What bus are we taking?" "Where do we get off?" "How long will we be on the bus?" I'm not quite sure how I lived through this experience but certainly God was protecting me. No child should feel like it's up to them to protect themselves but that is how I felt when I was with Daddy especially when he was using alcohol or drugs.

As a child, it was confusing and scary. Like all kids, I just wanted everything to be okay. I just wanted my Daddy to love me. Though I had no control over the things going on around me, they deeply impacted me. To this day, they impact how I deal with those around me, my ability to love unconditionally and even how I view myself. Am I worthy of forgiveness and love though I am deeply flawed? After all, if Daddy didn't love me enough to be completely in my life, who else will? Will I ever feel like I am good enough?

With Daddy gone for much of my childhood, it was up to Mum to raise my brother, sister and myself on her own. I like to think that I became a bit of a helper during this time in my life. Mum worked and went to school which meant that I was often left in charge.

Looking back perhaps dealing with the upheaval of my dad's substance abuse instilled in me a sense of accountability and the need to protect. I helped pack lunches, ensured siblings got to school and even started dinner. This responsibility brought out my underlying bossy nature and need to control especially when I wasn't listened to. Perhaps the accountability and responsibility were too much for one so young, but what choice did we have?

Faith and religion were a big part of my growing up. This added a sense of stability and provided a good moral compass. I began to realize things weren't normal. Like most kids, I sometimes strayed and got into trouble. I'm not sure when Mum began to attend The Worldwide Church of God but it was the only church I remember from my childhood. There were many instances when the support from church members provided a much-needed life preserver. It meant that when we had to leave because Daddy was out of control, Mum could turn to our church community. It meant that I had friends that went to the same church and had the same beliefs but that was only one day a week. It also meant that we had a different religion and kept the Old Testament Holy Days and Festivals. I was different not only because I was half the size of my peers but also because my family's religion was different. At the beginning of grade three, we moved to Scarborough Crescent in Port Coquitlam, BC. I went to school at Mary Hill Elementary just around the corner from our little crescent. Around Christmas time, Mum lined us up and gave each of us a note. "Kids, these notes are to be given to your teachers today." "They are to excuse you from participating in the Christmas play." All I wanted to do was fit in which was very difficult when my parents were divorced, I was tiny and had a different religion. I took that downright dastardly note and threw it on the muddy wet path as I made my way to school. Some helpful girls that were walking behind me picked up my discarded note and returned it to me. That should have been a sign. A sign which I missed. When I got to school, I threw my note in the trash. Let's just say that the remainder of the week was amazing. I participated in the Christmas play preparations and sang Christmas Carols at the top of my lungs. I knew it was wrong to disobey my Mum and that what I was doing went against what I had been taught. Fitting in with my peers seemed so much more important at the time.

At the end of the week, I arrived home with David and Carolyn. Mum was waiting for us and sent me directly to my room while my brother and sister got their after-school snack. When she finally came into the room, she towered over me as I sat on my bed with my legs dangling over the side. "Colette, did you give your teacher the note like I asked?" "Yes, I put it right in her hand, Mum!" In one split second my Mum grew into the biggest fire breathing dragon I had ever seen. I swear she had horns and a tail! Fire roared out of her mouth, "WHY did your Principal call wanting to know why David and Carolyn could not be in the play but you could?" I sat in front of my dragon Mum with tears streaming down my face. Her disappointment and anger at my lie were palpable and hung heavy in the air. "I'm sorry I'm sorry!" "I just wanted to fit in, no one likes me and our religion is STUPID!" Thankfully my Mum became my Mum once more and the dragon disappeared. She put her horns and tail away and her fiery breath subsided. My lesson was learned. I had to stand in front of my class and tell them why I could no longer partic-ipate in the play and how my religion was different than theirs. Part of surviving childhood is learning to stand up for who you are and your beliefs even if they are dictated by your parents at the time. I still struggle with this at times. The need to be liked and fit in can be a powerful hurdle to overcome.

One summer, Mum put us all in a day camp. Putting us in day camp meant that we were supervised while Mum worked and went to school. I remember feeling scared that I had to travel on the public bus with my siblings all by ourselves. It was a long bus ride but I was well prepared. Mum always made sure that I knew what to do. I was tiny so it was easy for me to be overlooked. I would often be at the bus stop with my siblings waiting to catch the bus to go home and .... Zoom .... the bus would go right by us. One afternoon this happened over and over again. I was panicked and desperate, it was starting to get dark. I was terrified to be out after dark and responsible for David and Carolyn. Finally, I practically stood in the street as the next bus approached, as if by my physical presence alone, I could will that bus to stop so we could get on and go home after camp. Somehow, we all stuck together and survived that summer ordeal.

A new man came into our lives when I was in grade six. Mum started dating a man she met at church. Fred was put through the ringer by three kids who didn't like him at all. "Mum, that man with the big nose is at the door again!" "Send him away. We don't like him!" Thankfully Fred was a patient man and Mum didn't listen to us. Fred was a humble man of slight stature who stuttered when we first met him. I remember him proudly walking down the aisle at church towards Mum in his dress pants that were too short. "Look at that. He's wearing floods!" We were utterly embarrassed by Fred and his attention. It didn't take long to realize that Fred was there to stay no matter how horrible we were to him. Mum and Fred got married just before I started grade seven and they have never looked back. It was nice to see Mum happy and loved even though at the time I thought Fred was a strange bird.

I refused to call Fred "Dad" even though I knew deep down it would make him happy. For all intents and purpose, he was Dad. He taught life lessons, took care of us and our Mum. One day after a particularly hard day at school, a day of being picked on, being called names and simply struggling to fit in, I arrived home. The only person there was Fred. Great! Not who I wanted to talk to. I poured out my heart to him anyway and he just listened. I don't remember his advice but I remember feeling better when

I left his workshop in the basement of our house. I was beginning to think Fred was okay. Finally, when Mum came home, I cried out my troubles to her too. "They call me Short Shit!" "No one likes me!" Her sage advice? "Just call them Big Turds." Now that made me laugh. The next day I came home and found Fred in his basement workshop. Instead of my surly grumble I said, "Hi Dad. Thanks for yesterday!" Fred's jaw dropped open. Not because I was somewhat nice but because I called him Dad. It surprised me just as much as it did him. I realized that I was setting a terrible example for my siblings and how unfair we had been to him. Besides, he earned it!

Fred was a roofer and eventually started his own roofing company which meant that we got to help out during the Summer. Fred paid well and I was willing to work hard. One summer I was saving up for a brand-new ghetto blaster. You know the kind the kids carried under their arm as they walked around? They were SO cool and I wanted one. They were $100.00 which was a fortune back then, especially to a kid like me. By the end of Summer, I had rough stained hands and enough money to make the big purchase. At the end of that Summer, we were done with work and heading home. I was so excited because it was the day! The day I was going to go and buy my ghetto-blaster. We arrived home and my sister was dancing like a crazy chicken around the front yard. "Go check out your room! Go look!" "Run and look!" Carolyn couldn't contain herself and she raced around clucking madly in excitement. I ran inside and raced up to my room. There on my bed was the biggest, shiniest black and silver ghetto blaster I had ever seen. It had all the bells and whistles. Mum and Fred had rewarded my hard work. Since then, I have always lived by the motto that hard work always pays off even if it doesn't seem like it at the time.

We all went to church and life was good. Like any community of people, there is the good and the bad. There were church camps, youth groups and a lot of fun times. There was a man named Don who none of the kids liked. In fact, we would often cross the aisle to avoid him if he was walking towards us. Kids simply just sense when something or someone is not okay. One Sunday there was a special gym day and I was excited because there was going to be gymnastics equipment set up. Mum and Fred sent us there with another church family and of course I felt responsible. Outside it was a normal rainy blustery Vancouver day but inside it was epic. I played on all the equipment and was having a blast. Carolyn was not having fun. She was sitting on the bleachers pouting. Carolyn didn't just pout, she had it down to a science. Her cheeks were so large that when she pouted her whole face hung down and her mouth gaped open. She told me she didn't feel well and wanted to go home. Of course, we couldn't just leave so I told her to go back to the bleachers and sit with our stuff. I went back and played on the uneven bars and beam. I was engrossed in what I was doing when I heard screaming. Everyone heard screaming. The hairs stood up on my arms because it was Carolyn. By the time I caught up to her, Don had her in his arms standing outside the large glass gym doors. The rain was bouncing off the glass doors as the wind gusted. Something wasn't right but as a kid you can't put it into words. I blasted through the gym doors and planted myself in front of Don with my hands on my hips. "Put her down. I'm here and I will take care of her!" Don stared me down as Carolyn screamed and adults walked by. "No, she needs an attitude adjust-ment. You can come with us if you want, Colette." We went back and forth for several minutes. Don just kept repeating himself. Adults from church kept walking by but no one stopped even when I pleaded with my eyes. "No, I won't come with you and she has no coat and no shoes! This isn't right!" I yelled and then when that didn't work, I tried to reason with him. Finally, I had enough and took one big step back and charged him. I ran right up the front of him, over Carolyn, and punched him in the nose. His glasses flew off his face and he dropped my sister. "RUN inside!" Carolyn picked herself up off the rain soaked concrete and dashed inside and I ran after her. Don called our parents immediately and told them that he had a slight discipline problem with me. Later when I was questioned, I couldn't explain why I did what I did. Like any kid, I mumbled, "I don't know." Looking back, I'm not sure what possessed me but I know that something bad would have happened if I hadn't been brave enough to stand up to an adult. Years later, it came out that Don was a child molester and the church elders didn't report it. He would latch onto single mothers and babysit their kids. I shudder to think how many kids were abused by this man who operated in the safety of the church as a Deacon. Many children don't escape childhood unscathed and thankfully Don didn't hurt my sister or me. From this experience, I learned to go with my gut. Always stand up to bullies and abusers even when you're pint size.

I was pint-sized my whole childhood. By the time I was eleven, David and Carolyn were the same size as me. I was three and five years older than them but my growth was so far behind my peers that I was always the kid sitting in the front holding the class sign in all the school photos. When I was in grade eleven, my Mum and Fred decided to address why I was so short and not developing at a normal rate. They took me to our primary care physician who had cared for our family for several years. I walked into Dr. Lim's office and she told me that I was there because my parents were concerned about my slow development and we were going to do some testing. Boy was I mad! I had been raised to believe I was normal and that there was nothing wrong with me. I was just a bit short! Okay, I was more than just a bit short, I was stuff her in a locker short. I was offended that my parents thought I was anything but normal. I had to do blood tests – a lot of blood was drawn – it seemed like buckets of blood. What I didn't know is that they were doing karyotype testing or genetic testing. This testing was to determine if an X chromosome was missing or partially missing. My tests came back showing that I was missing parts of an X chromosome. This is called Turners Syndrome or TS and it can come with a lot of different medical needs depending on what type of TS you have and how your genetically faulty chromosome is impacted. Unfortunately, it was too late for growth hormone therapy but I started hormone replacement therapy in order to continue with puberty as it had slowed down and was almost non-existent. Estrogen and Progesterone were needed to keep my bones and uterus healthy. Even with early intervention, almost all women with TS are unable to have children without medical intervention. I always thought I would have kids of my own but now I knew better. All this was crazy stuff for a teenage girl. I tried to brush it off and went on with things. I think it bothered my Mum more than me. She felt guilty even though this isn't an inherited disease but I felt relieved that there was an answer to my short stature and stalled puberty. For me, TS means I have an issue with visual-spatial learning and my hearing. Let's just say, learning how to drive was not easy for me. It involved Fred sitting beside me on the front bench seat of the car with his hand on the steering wheel as I tried to navigate down the road. Mum only braved my driving once and that didn't go well either. When it came time to take my driving test for the first time, I panicked and the tester, Black Bart, failed me before I even exited the parking lot. I persisted and eventually got my license when I was in my mid-twenties. Today I am a proficient driver and value all navigation devices so I don't get turned around and lost.

Only 1% of Turners pregnancies reach full term which means I am a bit of a miracle. Most TS pregnancies end up being spontaneously aborted and many times the grief-stricken parents never know why. I am one of the lucky ones. I am relatively healthy and other than my short stature, visual spatial issues and hearing loss, I am rocking it. Nothing is insurmountable. Today I view things with the perspective of what is possible instead of what isn't possible. All the struggles have left me with a glass half full attitude.

Mum and Fred's relationship and love was the glue that ensured I was able to overcome and mature into a productive adult. Over time, Fred became Dad and helped Mum finish raising us. They even added two more to the brood. Life wasn't always easy but we had what we needed and we were happy.

As I grew into adulthood, I had no idea how much my relationship and experiences with my biological dad, Mike, would impact my view of relationships and men. Despite the stability of the later years of my childhood, these early experiences would impact my decision making in my first marriage. I had seen the physical abuse growing up but I didn't recognize the emotional abuse and the toll that took on my Mum. This was relived in my first marriage. I met this attractive blond-haired, blue-eyed man when I was in my mid-twenties. He seemed like a good person who cared about me and would take care of me. His name was David and he even seemed to like me! Liking me seemed to be my first criteria to any developing relationship at the time. I quickly fell in love with his charm and good looks. I didn't see the signs of control and manipulation. The first warning sign was that he blamed his parents for everything and didn't have a relationship with them. The second warning sign was that although he was liked by others and had friends, he would often belittle me or tell me what I needed to work on when we were alone. This was all done in the name of helping me to "improve" as a person and a partner. We got married when we were both 29. I was in love and boy was he a keeper! What I didn't know was that he was not who he seemed to be. He was using drugs and cheating. I had no clue! We moved from Vancouver, British Columbia to Calgary, Alberta to start our married life and it was always a struggle. It would be my fault if I couldn't make money magically appear. It was my fault if I didn't make and pack his lunch just right. It was definitely my fault if the house wasn't clean.

He was good at manipulating, gas lighting and making me feel like everything was my fault. When Harry Potter was released, I really wanted to see it and begged him to take me. We went to the movie and I was enjoying it. The theatre was packed, the popcorn was buttery and I just knew the movie would be epic. About half an hour into the movie, he grabbed me by my arm and physically dragged me out of the theatre. "Why are you so stupid wasting my time with a kids movie!" I was so shocked that I couldn't respond. All I could do was follow him out like a lost puppy. Not only was I humiliated and confused but I was apologizing for something that wasn't my fault.

When I had all four of my wisdom teeth removed, David was not there for me at all. He had one of his friends pick me up and drop me off for the extraction procedure because he had to be at work. Once I was in recovery, he was called to come and pick me up and take me home. It is important that there is supervision for at least the first few hours after being knocked out when you have your wisdom teeth removed. Nope, that didn't happen for me. David had to go back to work so he left me alone. I had no water, no soft food near the bed ... nothing. I fell asleep. When I woke up, I was incredibly sick and needed water and food. I called David and he was mad I was interrupting his day. I ended up crawling to the kitchen to get yogurt and water. I sat on the floor until I felt like I could stand up. Looking back, I was lucky nothing happened to me during the first few hours of recovery. There were many times I would find marijuana hidden in the house but I couldn't say anything without causing a fight. I encouraged him to have a relationship with his parents as he really didn't have one with them. In fact, he didn't even invite them to our wedding which I know made his mother terribly sad. When we would go visit his parents, he would talk to me under his breath, "I'm going to leave you when we get home." His favorite thing to do was to mock me until I cried and then belittle me for being weak and crying. "You're getting fat, how can you eat that popcorn!" I was a size 4. A size FOUR! In the end, this relationship turned me into someone that I didn't like…let alone love. I became someone that I couldn't stand to be around. All I did was work, eat and sleep. I felt that because I wasn't beaten that it wasn't abuse. After all, in my early years, I equated abuse with physical beatings. I witnessed this more than once as I watched Mike hurt my Mum or threaten to hurt her.

I just wasn't strong enough to face the inevitable head on. In fact, I didn't really talk to anyone about what was going on. I was too embarrassed and ashamed. Though my family knew what was going on, it was something we didn't really discuss. Carolyn and I have a sister book that she bought and during this time we would write letters in the sister book and mail it back and forth to one another. She was struggling as well and feeling overwhelmed with work and finding her way in her marriage. I was struggling to break free of an abusive marriage. Her letter in our sister book on December 30, 2000 was telling. Below is an excerpt of her letter to me.

Dear Col, (cauliflower, levesq-el-head, snobette, my true sister friend)

The year in review: We worked like dogs at our jobs both you and I. Why? Because we're so bloody loyal ... almost to our own detriment. How many times did I feel like quitting and staying home to raise a family for a while? But alas, I'm too responsible to do anything too crazy like that! What about you? You're holding down two jobs and volunteering? Is it in you, my dear sister, to make a big change for your future happiness? I've always felt you were able to do this/make a big decision. You are much stronger than I. Did you know that you're worth so much more than what you're getting now? Someone else besides me must know this too!

Carolyn – XO

What Carolyn didn't realize is that her letter in our sister's book was timely and powerful. I was working two jobs and volunteering in order to stay out of the house and away from the emotional abuse. Her letter helped give me courage to hang on. It many ways it was the catalyst for me leaving Canada and moving to the United States in 2001.

My marriage was abysmal and I was isolated in many ways from friends, family, and even myself. I really didn't have many friends. I was living a lie. I found it hard to be honest and truthful with myself and what I was dealing with. It was far too scary and besides who wants to fail at marriage? Most of it was my fault according to my husband. No matter what Carolyn thought, I simply wasn't brave enough and I didn't know how I would survive if I left.

Sometime during all of this upheaval, I met Doug online in a chat room. I know what you are thinking. She has lost her mind! You wouldn't be wrong. Doug was kind and calm. He was the only person who I was completely honest with about what was going on in my relationship. Everyone else either thought I was brave for staying, ignored what was going on or simply didn't talk about it. Doug told me real men don't act like that. Well DUH! What I was experiencing in this marriage was not love. Though it was not the best thing to begin a relationship when I was married – I desperately needed to feel good. I'm not sure if it was the simple conversations and getting to know someone on that level without all the emotional issues or if it was a life-raft I was clinging to but I went with it. This meant lying to my husband, to Doug and to my family. I was hiding everything that was going on in one way or another. This meant making things sound better than they were, downplaying things, coloring things to make myself look better or simply not saying anything at all. Though I was intermittently staying with a friend, there were times when I was bullied back into the marital home. I didn't tell Doug this as I was certain he would wash his hands of me. I had been "stuck" for a long time and didn't know how to get unstuck!

One day, I finally had enough and gave my notice at work, called Doug and told him I was coming to Denver and made plans to run away. That is what it felt like to me…running.

I couldn't force myself to face it any other way. When my husband left the house, I packed two bags with a few belongings and left my dog Buster with the friend I was intermittently staying with. I made my way to the airport and nervously boarded a plane. I had a one-way ticket thanks to Doug…no strings attached. Without a word to friends or family, I left Canada and headed to the United States. Was I brave or being ridiculously unsafe? I know I scared my family by disappearing for a time. I didn't want my husband to find me. I was scared to be found and humiliated or worse bullied into returning. I knew that would be the final death of who I was at my core. Thankfully Doug turned out to be good man who loves me unconditionally. Today he is truly my best friend and a wonderful husband. He has been there for me through all the crazy ups and downs that my relocation to the U.S. has brought to our lives. Divorce, getting married, green card, buying our first home together and citizenship.

Over the years, my life has settled into a semblance of normal. I have a great family life filled with a terrific husband, two amazing step-daughters, grandkids and a beautiful extended American family. No woman has ever felt so blessed and reinvented. Though life is good, no one has heard from my biological dad. I refer to him as Mike when I talk about him now that I am an adult as he hasn't earned the title, "'Dad" and I've outgrown Daddy. Though I believe he loved me, he certainly didn't raise me. I often worried that he would be found dead in a ditch somewhere all alone due to his lifestyle. Mike finally showed up at a Hospital in Vancouver Canada. He was very ill but refused to let the Hospital staff call his family. When he finally lapsed into a coma, it was out of his hands and the hospital was able to reach out to family. When the hospital contacted family, we were told that when Mike showed up, all he had on him was a small bag with a few personal items: his guitar and a small television. There was not much hope for recovery. He was in kidney and liver failure, his body septic from all the abuse he had subjected it to.

My Levesque family decided to meet up in Vancouver and rally around Mike. The next day I found myself at Denver International

Airport waiting to board a plane. When I arrived in Vancouver, Canada, it was bittersweet. The wonderful feeling of being surrounded by family during this time is a blessing.

I was nervous to see Mike because after all of this time, I don't know how to feel about him anymore. The next morning, David, Carolyn and I showed up at the hospital and walked into his room. I didn't even recognize him. He was this tiny little man. He had no hair, no teeth, he was so…old looking. Like an empty shell, a small visage of that large scary man from my childhood.

Thankfully, he did recover and ended up being around for several more years. This allowed time for many phone calls and letters. I am thankful he was there when my Grandmere passed away and had the chance to say goodbye. He was able to develop healthier relationships with his kids and grandkids. I was distanced and insulated during his recovery because I lived in the United States.

In 2014, my husband Doug and I took a trip home to Canada to visit family and friends. It was a reunion of sorts because it has been so long since I'd been back to Canada. Mike was able to be part of this experience. It turned out to be the last time I would see him. My favorite memory from this trip was a family gathering Carolyn organized. She invited a houseful of people most we hadn't seen for a long time. I was excited and a bit nervous to see Mike. When Mike roared up on his motorcycle, I knew it was him as soon as I heard the rumble of the bike. That evening as the sun started to set, Mike brought out his guitar. As we sat around in a circle the crowd called out requests. Mike was center stage and loving it. We didn't care if we could sing or not…we just sang our hearts out. To see Mike having so much fun entertaining a crowd was amazing to watch. Mike was an AMAZING entertainer!

I got the call at work on August 11, 2016. My brother called to tell me Mike died. Then my Auntie Denise called. All I could think about was that it was terrible that I hadn't made more time to visit him. The truth was that all I could manage was phone calls and letters. I was a bit stunned. I had never lost a parent before and such as Mike was, he was still my dad. That day I finished up a project with a deadline at work, was the Toastmaster at a meeting and then I finally went home. I acted as if something monumental hadn't happened. I finally called Carolyn on the way home. She asked, "Do you want me to send you a picture of him?" Crying with her on the phone helped ground and connect me to the experience of losing a parent I had such an ambivalent relationship with. Seeing a picture of Mike at peace was strange, but helpful.

Another trip home, this time for a funeral was planned. I'm thankful that Carolyn was there to manage everything and that she had the Levesque's to lean on. We spread Dad's ashes near Grandpere and Grandmere Levesque which was very emotional for me. Looking back, Carolyn managed to make things easy for me and take on the burden of my inability to be one hundred percent present. I got to fly in with Doug, participate as needed, deliver a speech and fly home. I realize now that I missed how much the Levesque's loved Mike and even when he was at his worst, they were there when he needed them. Even my Dad Fred and Mum were there at Mike's memorial along with my youngest sister Kathleen. The craziest thing is that Dad was the first one to speak because no one wanted to step up. "I want to thank Mike for messing up so that I had the opportunity to have Karen and her kids in my life, you missed out Mike." Dad used humor and grace to say what I was thinking and then he sat down. At that moment, I couldn't have been prouder or more amazed that he understood all of the brokenness and loved anyway. Mum had to face all the resurfacing emotions that dealing with the family of her abuser brought up. I am not sure how she was able to find the strength to be there for us during this time but I'm grateful she was there by my side. Her strength is in her forgiveness and I hope I can continue to grow into half the woman she is.

I was amazed that the life of a man who ensured I grew up too fast and had to face things no child should have to experience could still generate a lesson of love. My husband was there through it all. A calm comfort in the storm who dealt with things perfectly. The lessons of love were left in bits and pieces all around me. The Levesque's, my parents, my husband, my sisters and brother, my niece and nephew … each was able to forgive and see love in their relationship with Mike.

How have I been able to get past all the challenges that my life experiences have placed before me? I'd like to think it hasn't been by chance or sheer luck. The truth is, there has been a lot of help along the way along with a little luck and a lot of perseverance. Afterall, no matter where you find yourself in life, no matter what challenges you face, it's the getting up and moving forward despite it all that defines who you truly are.

Today, I love myself with all my strengths, faults and flaws more and more each day.

Colette Smith is a transplanted Canadian, avid Toastmaster and storyteller. She has participated in Moth Story Slam as well as The Story Project based out of Colorado Springs.

She is a survivor of domestic abuse whose focus is sharing her story in order to inspire others to forgive, overcome and learn to love again.

When she isn't on stage speaking or writing you can find her scuba diving with her husband, Doodles, somewhere in Florida.

CHAPTER 4
ERIN

Postpartum Depression
Finding Hope Amongst the Loss

My mind draws a blank as I stare at the word *postpartum*. I am lost in finding my thoughts as they race through my mind. I never really understood the word, its meaning or what it meant for those who were experiencing it. What were they truly going through? I am still not quite sure what it all means as I find it hard to comprehend that I am suffering from postpartum. Do I dare, add the word depression to it? I don't. For me, I grew up around depression and I swore I would "never" suffer. However, that's just not fair – it's not fair to me, nor is it fair to those who have battled with it in their own lives.

I have always been one to find the positive and keep going even when I am in the lowest valley with what seems like an impossible climb. I truly believe it is in the core of my being to be upbeat and happy go lucky. However, even I have my moments of despair, sadness, grief and moments of confusion. When I don't really understand the purpose of my struggles.

I find myself just after a month of a devastating loss. A loss, I had no idea I was going to experience. I woke up on December 8, 2019 with an explosion of pain in my lower left pelvic region. I was in agony. As I tried taking inventory of the situation – I was silently weeping and the tears slowly carved paths down my cheeks. As I pressed firmly with my left hand where the explosion took place, I was confused of the seriousness of the situation that was unfolding. However, it would be half a day later when I would grasp the reality of my fate.

At 1:48 am, I was awoken out of a deep sleep and found myself in my bed with my beloved kitty, Kodak, next to me– staring at me–wondering why I was suddenly awake and in extreme pain. Zach, my husband, had been working 14-hour days and had fallen asleep on the couch watching *Star Trek*. I sat in my bed for what seemed like forever, as my breath was stolen from me with every passing minute. As I gathered my thoughts, I decided it would be best to calmly and quietly make my way downstairs to wake up my husband.

With every step I took, the pain intensified. It took everything out of me as I lowered myself down each step closer to the living room. However, I never made it. I got to the landing, halfway down our staircase, and screamed in agony. My husband was up before I knew it–locking eyes with me as my sight was blurred with tears.

I explained, there's been an explosion and I am in extreme pain. He looked at me with fear and sadness as he rushed to my side and he asked, "What do I do?". I responded through my cries, "I don't know!"

He helped me back into the room and into bed. I sat there in pain and confusion in the middle of the night. He suggested we go to the emergency room and I shook my head no – knowing damn well it was a stupid response.

I had been going through the Financial Peace University class of Dave Ramsey's and I just thought about how much this was going to cost. The flash of what the assumed bill would be. Though I had our initial emergency fund set up, I didn't want to go.

I explained to Zach, we couldn't afford it.

So, we both reached for our phones. As I dialed my sister's phone number, my husband called his parents. My sister didn't answer. I called my infertility specialist and I could barely speak through the pain. I was finally able to tell the nurse on call that there had been an explosion and I was in an immense amount of pain. She responded with what seemed like a laugh and a, "I have never heard of that, good luck!"

More confused than ever, there was just no way I was pregnant. I mean, the nurse asked me and it wasn't even a thought. Afterall, I had a period on November 17 – less than half a month ago. I was three days late, but it came.

My phone rang. It was my sister.

I once again explained the situation. She used to work in an OBGYN clinic, so I thought maybe she would have some insight.

She gave me a couple scenarios of what could be happening. First, I could possibly have a cyst and it had ruptured. Second, I was pregnant and I was losing the baby or third, we have no idea.

It couldn't be the first or second—or could it?

I asked her what I should do? She advised that I should go to the emergency room. However, if I really didn't think I could afford it, or I was sure I wasn't pregnant, then the best thing to do would be to take some Tylenol and try to get some sleep, wait until morning and go to an urgent care. I chose the latter option.

As my husband came back into the room after speaking to his parents, I told him about the conversation I just had with my sister. I explained to him that we should wait until morning and try to get some sleep. He went downstairs to fetch me some Tylenol and was back at my side. As he handed me the Tylenol and some water, I explained that regardless of what I say in the morning, he has to take me in to urgent care or the emergency room, no matter what.

I took the Tylenol and I did my best to fall asleep. I drifted in and out of sleep with the rhythm of the pain that kept haunting me through the night. With my left hand still placed where the explosion had taken residence. Pressing it or holding my hand there comforted me in a strange way. Almost as if, I knew something was seriously wrong and I just needed to bide my time.

7:30 am came and I slowly began to wake up from my slumber. As time crept on, I got up and I got myself dressed. My husband and I headed out the door around 8:30 am. No food, no water, just slow steps and getting into the car on the front passenger side. My husband got into the driver's seat and slowly backed out of our garage. The pain was coming and going and I just didn't feel good, not in the slightest.

Something was seriously wrong and I needed to get help immediately. We made it to the Urgent Care only a few minutes away. As we stepped up to the counter, I took out my insurance card and started handing it to the front desk staff member. As, she glanced at my insurance card, she looked at me and said, "We don't take Bright Health." My husband stepped in and said that this was urgent and the Bright Health website states clearly on the home page that in case of an urgent medical related issue, it will cover the costs. As he pulled up the website as proof of coverage, the woman began to argue with my husband. My pain grew and my patience was diminishing with every breath I took.

I told my husband that we should just go. As we turned to leave, the patients that were waiting in the lobby started slowly lifting their heads to take a look at the one being turned away. My husband was furious and I just wanted to get out of there.

We made our way back to the car. I slowly got in and pulled up the list for the nearest in network Emergency Room. It was about 10 minutes away. We made our way there and walked in. We were the only ones there which meant it shouldn't be long before I could be seen.

As we checked in at the front desk, we shared our story from a year earlier of how we had been trying to conceive and how it ended up as an ectopic pregnancy (a pregnancy in which the fetus develops outside the uterus, typically in a fallopian tube), a loss which resulted in an exploratory surgery. We were trying to pass the time and keep my mind occupied. We kept sharing with the front desk lady and she was sweet and seemed to actually care. We shared how the surgery revealed many different issues and our hopes were still high to eventually conceive a child of our own.

As quickly as we walked in, we were being brought back to a room. Oh, Thank God, I felt safe. Surely, they would be able to figure out what was going on and what caused the explosion inside my body. By this point, it was around 9:30 am. They checked me in, had me fill out paperwork and put on a gown.

They took my vitals and began assessing the situation by asking question after question. The doctor came in, looked at me and said, "Tell me what's going on, what brings you in today?" After I gave him the step-by-step explanation, the doctor followed it with the question they always ask females, "Is it possible you are pregnant?" I answered quickly, "No, I mean, well we've been trying, but we struggle with infertility and I have had my period." The doctor nodded his head and told me that he wanted to run a few tests to rule out anything and one of those was a pregnancy test. He left the room and the nurse came back in to take my blood for several tests and to give me a cup to collect a urine sample. They needed to first rule out a pregnancy or the other option which would mean that I was indeed pregnant.

I took the cup, went into the bathroom and followed the steps to catch a "clean sample", twisted the cap back on and handed it to the nurse when I was finished. Sitting in the hospital bed, tired, hungry and scared, I tried to distract myself with my phone while my husband sat exhausted from just finishing up a 3 month stretch of work that required 12-14-hour days, 7 days a week. We waited for what seemed like days, but in all reality was probably more like an hour. The doctor returned with the results from the urine test. He took a seat and as he raised his eyes to meet mine. He slowly lowered my file onto his lap. I knew what he was about to say. I could feel it with my entire being. As he began to speak, the words pierced my heart as they were spoken carefully. The doctor told me I was in fact pregnant and my numbers were fairly high, which meant I was a few months along. Therefore, they needed to do a few more tests to show exactly what was going on. I gasped for air as I realized I was losing yet another baby that I didn't even have a chance to celebrate. It was confirmed, but as a woman, you know your body. As reality hit me, I was devastated. The tears fell from my eyes and I knew there was yet more bad news on the horizon. I suddenly found myself in a nightmare I was all too familiar with. It had happened before—a year and one week to the day in 2018. I could see the sadness in my husband's exhausted eyes and as the doctor departed the room, I wept.

This was the last thing my husband needed, to be in a hospital, worried about me and trying to put on a brave face. So, I told him to go home, check on the cats and get coffee or some rest while they ran more tests. I could handle it because I had to. After all, I was the patient and there was nothing my husband could do until we knew more.

He kissed me goodbye, told me he loved me and left to take care of a things at home. I laid there, sad, hopeless and heartbroken. I didn't want to jump to any conclusions but I just knew it wasn't good.

A woman walked in, she was the sonographer and explained to me that she would be doing a vaginal ultrasound to see what was going on. As violating as those exams feel, I was relieved that the tests were being done. As she inserted the cold, hard plastic wand, I took a deep breath—once again remembering how familiar it all felt over a year ago when I was told I had lost my first baby. I did my best to breathe, hold back the tears and try not to jump to any conclusions. I watched her as she looked at the screen, taking measurements and doing her best not to allow any expression to draw upon her face. I listened with each click of the keys on the keyboard, trying to numb the pain I was in. Lying there, being examined and knowing that she couldn't tell me a thing. However, that didn't keep me from asking her questions. I worked up the courage and between probes, asked her, "Do you see anything?" She looked at me, answered and said, "There is something, but the radiologist will need to confirm and I really can't tell you anything." That was enough for me. I knew it was bad, I just didn't know how bad. Here I was, lying in a hospital bed, with my legs spread as the sonographer was doing her job and couldn't tell me anything. She apologized with every twinge of pain I expressed as she probed to make sure she was getting a complete and clear picture of what was happening. The test felt like hours, though it was about 30 minutes. She finished, removed the wand and allowed me to close my legs. As she pushed back the sonagram cart, she told me the radiologist will read the results and the doctor will be in shortly.

Again, it was a hurry up and wait situation. Alone in the hospital, I was left to my thoughts. I texted my husband occasionally as our conversation consisted of me asking him to bring my charger. He let me know about the cats and how he needed to deal with a cat pee emergency because Pumba, who was 19, had a hard time making it into the litter boxes and occasionally would give up trying, which meant accidents. He also wanted to make sure he cleaned the litter boxes for our other three fur babies. I told him that I had spoken to the doctor and that I needed them to call our current infertility specialist for options and that we have to terminate the pregnancy as it was ectopic. Before my husband could get word in, I told him that they are talking about administrating the drug Methotrexate again and how I asked to see the images of the sonagram, which they did show me, though there wasn't much to see. I just knew I was pregnant with another ectopic and it would result in another loss. I have no idea what thoughts went through my husband's mind at that moment, but as his text came through, I knew he was being brave for me as it read, "I'm so sorry honey" I responded with, "This sucks. We can get Prego, but not with a viable one. Feel broken." He didn't understand what I was trying to tell him. I just knew that our path to parenthood was not going to be easy. I wrote him back, "We can get pregnant but not with a viable pregnancy. Ectopic has been the norm. It sucks." I waited as the three little dots blinked across the screen and as the messages came through, I did my best to hold back the tears. "Maybe it's possible, but I want to ask my grandpa for help with IVF. If we can do that, it's our best shot honey." I laid there, devastated, angry and heart broken and mostly scared of what was going to happen. I picked up the phone, to text my husband, I wrote, "Ok, but now we have to wait for my body to terminate and heal, longer than last time." I knew there was more to it than that because at this point, I haven't heard what our fertility specialists thought needed to be done. My husband's response was short and simple, "Okay."

I knew my husband was almost done taking care of things at home and he would soon be by my side in the hospital. So, I watched a little TV and tried to rest. I was hungry, yet wasn't allowed to eat as there was the possibility of what was to come.

They kept denying me food and it got to a point where I didn't even care anymore.

My husband was back by my side around 2:00 pm. Just in time for the doctor to come back after speaking with the doctor on call at the fertility center. He informed us that the doctor on call suggested skipping the Methotrexate and going into emergency surgery as she felt that my life was in danger, especially since there was an explosion, extreme pain and bleeding. She didn't think Methotrexate was the right protocol for the situation. Regardless of which path we chose, we needed to be discharged from the current emergency room and admitted into an actual hospital that had the resources needed for either option.

As we waited for them to discharge us, our concern for my life became apparent. I was in a state of shock with everything I had just been told. I had a very difficult decision to make between the two choices I was given. As we walked out of the hospital, I was overwhelmed with a sense of numbness. I thought to myself, "Wait, I'm pregnant? Wait, I am a few months along? Wait, I had no idea? Wait, it's ectopic? Wait, my life is in danger? Wait, I have to make a decision. How do I know which one to make? Wait, wait, wait!" This can't be happening, no, not again. My head was spinning and my world was falling apart.

My husband helped me into the car and he drove me to an in-network hospital, Avista. When we arrived, I made my way to a chair while my husband went up to the emergency department's front desk to check me in. I was still in severe pain and just wanted to go home, but I knew that was the last thing that was going to happen.

As I wrestled with the thoughts, I was interrupted by being called back and taken to a room within the emergency department. The nurse asked me what was going on and we explained the nightmare. When the doctor came in, he expressed that he thinks Methotrexate would do the trick. Sorry to say, I am not the main act in the magic show and I wasn't about to take my chances. I explained that I didn't feel well and that I had an ectopic before in which they administered that drug. I told him how awful I felt afterwards and they had to do surgery a few months later anyway. The doctor then decided that he needed another opinion, a doctor that was qualified in the area of reproduction, an OBGYN. Well, she was upstairs delivering a baby and as soon as she was done, she would be in to examine me. We waited.

It was around 4 pm at this point and I was exhausted, hungry and I just wanted to do what was best. I had so many emotions and I hadn't even called my dad yet. I knew we needed to; I just didn't want to worry him. After all, I am his little girl and he experienced all of this first hand a year prior. Before I called him, I wanted us to have the information so we could tell him everything we knew. My husband had been keeping in touch with his parents. I figured he would as he needed to talk to someone, because he knew he needed to also be brave for me as I was trying to be brave for him, but inside, we both were falling apart.

The doctor finally arrived and we explained what was going on, how I had surgery last year due to an ectopic and how our fertility clinic doctor felt that this time surgery was necessary. The OBGYN thought the Methotrexate would do the trick. I insisted she call the fertility clinic and talk the doctor on call and pull up my records from the surgery the year prior as it was done at the very same hospital I was now lying in. She agreed and excused herself from the room. As she did that, the phlebotomist came in to take blood to run more tests, even though this had all just been done.

My husband already knew what path he wanted me to take. He insisted that we just do the surgery, but I hesitated. I was scared and I didn't know what to do. I didn't want to be cut open again and I didn't want to take the Methotrexate only to need surgery a few months later. I didn't want what was happening to be happening. So, I told my husband to call Mama Ellen! Mama Ellen is a friend, client and honestly, she's my Colorado Mom. I trust her. She has been there since I started on the journey towards motherhood. She was there during the first loss, the surgery and the recovery. I knew she would tell me what I needed to do.

My husband, Zach, picked up the phone and called her. She answered and Zach explained everything. He then asked, "What should we do?" He sat and listened. He looked up at me and I knew, I knew she said surgery. He handed the phone to me. As I brought the phone to my ear, I said, "Hi." Mama Ellen spoke with such gentle compassion and said, "You need to have the surgery!" I knew she was right as was my husband, but I was scared. I was scared because my life was in danger. I was losing a baby I didn't even know I was carrying. I knew my husband was scared and yet he was being so brave. I had a quick conversation with Mama Ellen and I said my goodbyes. I handed the phone back to my husband and said, "Guess I am having surgery." I turned away and cried.

Just then the doctor came in and she explained that she had spoken to the doctor on call at the fertility clinic and had advised her that surgery was necessary to remove the ectopic pregnancy and to save my life. "Save my life?" Those are words that I didn't like hearing. Was I in that much danger? After all the things from the explosion, to finding out I was pregnant, to losing it and now needing surgery, it was a lot. Yet, it wasn't just surgery, it was life-saving emergency surgery. As she spoke, I listened intensely to the words, "We are going to operate and I have one job and one job only, to go in, remove the ectopic pregnancy, save your life and get out."

She followed it up by informing us that I will more than likely lose my tube. Oh, to throw more wood on the fire of infertility, natural conception and IUI (Intrauterine Insemination...aka, artificial insemination) were no longer options for us to have a family. Only IVF (In Vitro Fertilization) would work. After that, she said surgery will be at or around 7 pm and they would begin to prep me shortly.

As she left, I knew we needed to call my dad. So, we did. Zach spoke to him first and explained what was going on and then handed me the phone. It was my Daddy on the other line, being him and telling me that everything was going to be alright. As I told him I loved him, I could hear the sadness in his voice. The tears must have been filling his eyes. He said he loved me back and quickly handed the phone to his friend. She said hello, we spoke for a brief moment and said goodbye. I handed the phone back to my husband. I let out a deep and saddened sigh. I was exhausted and hadn't had anything to eat for over 24 hours. My hunger pains left hours ago as the sadness took over.

Lying in the hospital bed with my husband by my side, I tried to put on a brave face. I failed. I couldn't anymore. I was tired, scared and I just wanted the nightmare to be over. It's the bravest

I have seen my husband. I knew he was exhausted and hadn't had much sleep. Behind his tired eyes, I could see his worry and concern for me. As I told him I was sorry, he reminded me that I had nothing to be sorry about. All he cared about was my life being saved. It's a scary thing when you face death. Knowing that if we hadn't gone to the hospital and I just let it go, I would probably not be here sharing my story of loss and love.

How many thoughts can go through one's mind at one time, millions? It was like I was watching someone else's life unfold before my eyes…as if I was watching a movie. Yet, I was the featured character and it was my life that was unfolding before me at a pace that was hard to keep up. As the thoughts were racing through my mind, it was like they were stuck on repeat.

So many things were thrown at me that day, that it was hard to take it all in. All the information was pushed aside from being pregnant, to losing the baby to focusing on surviving. I laid there and just allowed myself to go numb, waiting as the big hand on the clock went from second to second and rounding the face of the clock once more. My eyes drifted from the clock to the hall to my husband. I found myself admiring my husband's face as I struggled to grasp my reality. My husband stayed busy, keeping in contact with family as I did my best to stay calm and rest. Before I knew it, the Anesthesiologist came in to talk to me before prepping me for surgery. It was almost time as the hands on the clock slowly ticked and tocked. I could hear each click with each minute passing. A little past 7:30 pm, I was being wheeled out of the room, telling my husband I loved him as tears rolled down my face. I was scared. It was time for me to be put under and my life to be put in the hands of the doctors. It's a humbling thought really, when you are facing death but know that you will survive if it's God's plan.

As we inched closer to the operating room, I prayed to God and told him that we needed to talk while the doctors did their job and that I needed to make it. We, God and I needed to have a conversation about me and how I had a lot more living to do and how I don't know what lies ahead as far as me being a mom. How, if I didn't have doubts before, I do now and how the little bit of hope I was holding on to, I wasn't sure if it was still there. I was devastated, angry and just exhausted. Exhausted from the previous years of trying, the ups, downs. Tired of trying to remain positive and scared to keep holding on to hope. Because at this point, I wasn't sure if there was any. I grew extremely tired as we reached the doors to the operating room where the surgery would take place. The last thing I remember is trying to hold onto a little bit of hope I had left while thinking of my husband as my eyes closed.

I am an optimistic person by nature. I was just wanting to make it through surgery even though I was scared of what news I would be given when I woke up. I just knew I had more things to do on Earth and prayed I would be given more days to live.

The next thing I remember is being in a dark room. I did not want to open my eyes but I was being abruptly awakened by the nurses and doctor who operated telling me to wake up. I was struggling coming out of anesthesia and they were talking to me. I was confused, "Where was I?" Slowly, opening my eyes to a nurse looking at me and repeating, "You need to breathe." As the nurse turned away, she said softly to another nurse, "We need to get her on oxygen. She's not breathing. Her lips are blue." As soon as she said that, there were tubes leading into my nose and oxygen flooding my airways. Meanwhile, a woman nurse was telling me to breathe through my nose. Waking up, I grasped my surroundings. The doctor approached me and explained that the surgery went great. She removed the ectopic and was sorry but she had to remove my tube as well. Yet, the most important thing she said came next. "We saved your life." I was very much in an agitated state waking up from the surgery. I was confused, angry, broken-hearted and given more bad news as expected, yet in all the chaos I was going to be okay. I lived.

I had been told before the surgery that it was likely and now it was certain. I had one remaining tube and it was in bad shape. She confirmed that in fact our only option to conceive a biological child would be IVF. My heart broke. I know that IVF is still an option or at least I hoped. At this point, I just wanted to sleep and escape my reality just for a moment. As I woke up even more, I became aware of the pain both physically and emotionally. There was a nurse there and she explained that they had a hard time getting me to come out of anesthesia along with difficulty breathing. It scared me. I told her; "I don't want to go home." She assured me that I would be staying overnight to be monitored as a precaution. If I recovered over night, I would be able to go home the following day. I was relieved. I just wanted to see my husband and go to bed. It had been a long day.

As they checked my vitals, they prepared for my transport into a room within the hospital where I would be monitored closely. As soon as I was settled into my room, my husband was able to be by my side. As I glanced at the clock, it was past 11 pm and we were both tired but relieved that I was going to be okay. My husband kissed me goodbye and told me he loved me. I stayed awake until I knew he made it home. The text came through at 11:47 pm it read "Home I love you." I wrote back, "I love you. Goodnight." As always, he responds back with "Goodnight I love you too." We texted a little longer and he expressed how he was taking tomorrow off and I simply responded with, "So glad you made me go." And an, "ok" in response to his taking the day off. His fear did come through in the next text that read, "We should have gone last night. Thank God we decided on the surgery." It was now the next day at 12:05 am, and, in my nature, I responded, "Yes I know. Sorry. I'm glad too." With his most forgiving nature, he simply writes back, "It's okay, I'm just so thankful you're alive."

I fell asleep after that but I had a hard time sleeping throughout the night. It was mostly because I was uncomfortable from the surgery, in an unfamiliar environment and being strapped to oxygen. Any one of those would make it hard for me to fall asleep. It didn't help that I had to use the bathroom every few minutes, or so it seemed. That, in itself, was a task. I was tired, weak and strapped to a line that was making sure I was getting enough oxygen. Every time I did want to get up, I was instructed to ask for help by dinging a nurse. I did, all night long.

After the sun began to rise, it was starting to take too long to get a nurse to assist me to the bathroom. Impatiently, I made the executive decision that as long as I took it slow and was careful, I could make it to the bathroom on my own. It would take less time with all the waiting and assisting that I could go to the bathroom and be back in bed before the nurse even stepped foot into my room. Did I mention, I am stubborn?

At 7:09 am, I received at text that I get most mornings from the love of my life and it simply says, "Good morning beautiful." It meant more to me on that morning because it meant I was alive. Though I still had to recover and focus on getting better, I knew that my husband was there to help me. As the minutes passed by, I was still in the hospital waiting to be released. They had me eat breakfast and by 10 am my Mama Ellen came by to check on me. She stayed a while and kept me in good spirits. She didn't stay too long. Before I knew it, she was leaving and my husband was there. He came to check on me and to find out when I may be able to go home. Still nothing. I told my husband there was no sense in him staying. We both knew he needed to take a nap. After all, he would be the one taking care of me once I did make it home and he needed to be well rested.

A couple hours later, the nurse made me take a walk down the hall. It didn't go so well. I made the comment that I felt like I was going uphill. After that, I was back in the hospital bed getting all my vitals checked once again. Turns out that my blood pressure was extremely low…ugh. Sometimes you just need to keep your mouth shut. I laugh at that sentence, because I am one that usually doesn't. This time, it kept me in the hospital longer than we originally thought. I just wanted to go home and be with my husband and four fur babies. Yup! Four fur babies, Taco, Kodak, Leela and Pumba. All cats, but all my babies. I missed them and I was honestly tired of lying in a hospital bed watching TV without any company.

By 4:00 pm on December 9, I was finally going home. I was so glad. I just couldn't wait to be home to see my beautiful fur babies and sleep. I knew it wouldn't be easy but at least I would be home.

My reality was different. Yesterday, I found myself in pain and did not know the cause. Now, 36 hours later, I was thinking about how an unknown pregnancy almost took my life. To think we could get pregnant, but not in the normal "make love" kind of way. Our only option laid in the hands of medical intervention and doctors who specialized in artificially fertilizing eggs – Invitro fertilization (IVF)…not so romantic. To top it off, being romantic or intimate meant protecting ourselves at all times. Even though we are married, protection was needed for the pure reason of the word. The word "protection" has taken on a whole new meaning when it comes to sex or intimacy within our relationship. It's not about the typical concerns but rather preventing pregnancy all together because if one little swimmer was to reach an egg and penetrate it, it could possibly end my life. For us, that doesn't turn us on in the least. However, first things were making it home and for me to rest, recover and grieve. Grieve for yet another loss. A loss that I didn't even know I had coming. A baby, I didn't know was conceived and a life I had to say goodbye to the moment I became aware of its existence.

I am not one that likes to just sit around and be lazy, yet here I was, post emergency life-saving surgery, bored out of my mind. I stayed in the guest room so I wouldn't disrupt my husband who is a light sleeper. That way, I could get some sleep without the cats, if needed. The next few days, I slept while my husband helped nurse me back to health. All I wanted to do was get back to my life. There was one problem…I had to recover first. A week went by and I was determined to get out of the house to distract my mind and heart by going to the store. I didn't realize how everyday activities wiped me out. I needed to give myself grace, so I did. I didn't get back to work until January 2020. A few people in my life thought that was too soon. They know that I am not one to stay down too long. By January 20, I was back to coaching clients and recovering slowly. I figured I had everything under control until my post-op appointment with my doctor to check on my surgical wounds and to discuss my next steps.

It was January 7, 2020. Time for my post-op appointment with the doctor who performed the surgery. I didn't know what would be discussed, so I decided that it would be best if my husband came with me. I went in thinking I was okay, that we would discuss the procedure and what she did. First, she took a look at the surgical sites and then she brought up my loss. Oh, that's right, I lost a baby. I was so focused on healing and moving on, getting back to life, that I pushed that down, way down. My eyes filled up with tears as we discussed the surgery, the loss and the fact that I was too high-risk for natural conception or even IUI. I was trying to be strong, hold back my tears and pretend that I really had no reason to grieve. After all, I didn't even know that I was pregnant until the day I found out I was losing it. She continued and informed us, just as she had in the emergency room on December 8, 2019, that our only option to have a biological child would be IVF. She was blunt, straight forward. I liked that. There was no fluff, no matter how hard the words would hurt. She continued to talk to me and I wept. I couldn't stop the tears. I kept looking at my husband. I was devastated. I was so focused on getting back to "life" that I forgot to mourn the life of the baby I had lost. My second pregnancy that I didn't even know about, one that I didn't get to acknowledge, I now had to morn. That's when the doctor told me that she believed I was suffering from *Postpartum Depression*. I was confused, "I thought Postpartum Depression was for those who gave birth and just didn't bond with their baby?" She went on to explain that Postpartum Depression can affect all women. Because I had now lost two ectopic pregnancies within a year of each other, she was confident I hadn't grieved the first loss and most certainly not the second. Her advice for me was to give myself grace. I should seek professional help in order to navigate these unknown waters. It felt like another blow, another failure on my part. *What did I do wrong?*

As a woman that seems to be our "go-to" question. Questioning what we did or didn't do? Sitting there, 6-weeks post-surgery, I was not only hurting, I was angry, confused and I could feel my heart breaking. I did everything I could to try to hold it together, yet the weight was too much to bear and all I wanted to do was wake up from this nightmare. I couldn't because I was living it; it was surreal. I just kept replaying the reel that I had been living, rewinding and fast-forwarding my life in the past three years. The past few months questioning all of it. Most of all, asking God to at least give me something. At this point, I felt that the hope I had was slipping away so quickly that I wasn't sure I would ever get it back. All I did know was I needed help. I decided to make an appointment to talk to a therapist that specialized in Postpartum Depression to help me wrap my head around all that has happened. I didn't know where to begin. A week later, on January 15, I had my first appointment. As I walked in to the doctor's office to check myself in, I had a sense of sadness come over me. I was sitting in the waiting room surrounded by moms-to-be and moms with their little ones. All I wanted to do was to get out of that waiting room. It seemed like forever, but finally my name was called. As I looked up, I saw a young lady with dark skin, brown eyes and long dark hair. She had a calmness about her. As I stood up and walked towards her, she extended her hand and I met it with mine and we exchanged hellos. I followed her back to an office where we could talk and discuss my concerns. The room was filled with a few desks, more office chairs than needed and a couch. It was not the most comforting room. In fact, it seemed more like a closet than anything else. Yet here I was, sitting on the couch across from a woman who I was to open up to about my loss and what I was experiencing. I sat there on the couch, still in my big winter coat, a stocking cap and holding my hands. I didn't know where to start. Was I to start from three years ago or the past six weeks? That day seemed like a blur. The one thing I do remember is just talking, while the tears filled up my eyes and I did my best to catch them before they fell off the curves of my cheeks. As I verbally expressed my deepest pains in regards to another great loss, I felt as if I was finally giving myself permission to be vulnerable…not only about my recent loss but my loss a year prior and everything in between. Finally, I felt safe to share my fears of what it means to lose and my fears of the journey I was on to become a mother. I had finally taken the first step to healing myself. It was exhausting. I wept during most of the appointment, but not once did I feel judged or shamed for what I was feeling. This young therapist met my gaze with eyes that were filled with kindness, sympathy and compassion. When she spoke at the end of our appointment, she assured me that I was in fact suffering from *Postpartum Depression*. Her recommendation would be therapy sessions where we could dive into my pain through talking and art therapy. She gave me my first assignment. I was to begin journaling in the morning and evenings to help me process my thoughts, dreams and feelings. I agreed to do so since I needed to start somewhere. We then set up my first appointment for a week later to begin my grieving and healing process. It gave me a little sense of control in a world that seemed to be crumbling before me.

My first therapy session was a week later on January 22. Of course, I showed up at the wrong location…oh goodness. So I rescheduled. Finally, my appointment was here and I was at the right location. As I walked into the center, I had a moment of imposter syndrome. I sat there doubting myself. Questioning if I really needed this or if I belonged? I tried to stop the rambling thoughts in my mind and allow myself to be okay with not being okay. Because I know myself pretty well, I realized it was my defense mechanism kicking in; trying to be strong, pretending that I could handle all that happened on my own. Yet my heart knew better. Our first session was really about getting to know one another. We established trust and discussed the therapies in which she would use to help guide me on my journey to find peace as I grieve my two pregnancy losses as well as any other grief that may come up for me. At the time, I wasn't sure what she meant, but it didn't take long to understand that as I was grieving the pregnancy losses. I was also grieving the idea of the ways to get pregnant that were no longer options. Learning this was eye-opening because I didn't realize that it was possible to grieve the idea of something that you thought was a possibility. Meaning, I was told by the doctor that my options I had before in means of getting pregnant were no longer available to me. If I was to ever conceive a child biologically, there was only one option, IVF. That was hard to hear and I wasn't sure how to navigate the emotions that this brought up.

As I continued therapy, I discovered a lot about myself. It, shouldn't have surprised me as therapy has a way of doing that. My therapy appointments not only gave me a safe place to be completely vulnerable but a sense of control when I felt everything else was out of my control. In my world, outside of therapy, I filled it up as much as possible to distract myself from the grief I was feeling. I tend to do that, until God says, "No more." I was doing pretty well distracting myself when I could and trying to get back to what I considered my normal life. That didn't last long, as my world got flipped upside down along with the rest of the world. On March 16, 2020 it was announced that the state of Colorado (which I live) was being drastically affected by a Pandemic which was caused by a Coronavirus known as COVID-19. We were informed by the Government that the state was being put on a "STAY AT HOME" mandatory order effective immediately. The COVID-19 Pandemic not only stopped Colorado in its tracks but the rest of the country and world. Everyone went into isolation and began to panic. Not only was I dealing with my two losses, grieving options that were no longer available to me to start a family, but now we were all thrown into isolation within our homes. Just when I thought I was getting a pretty good handle on my life, therapy and everything in between, it all stopped overnight.

On that same day, I had to shut down my business and shift my in-person therapy sessions to online while living everyday within the four walls of my house. I was thankful though; I had my husband who worked from home along with my four fur babies. I was not completely alone. It was a tough adjustment. Here I was in the middle of my grieving/healing process that I felt was progressing nicely with and now having to navigate that through a worldwide Pandemic. My mind did a complete shift, from grieving the loss of both my pregnancies, to my most recent one and thanking God that I wasn't pregnant during a Pandemic we knew nothing about except that it was caused by a virus and was very dangerous.

I continued my weekly therapy through an online portal. It definitely created a different dynamic. The first couple sessions, I would sit in my office, but it just didn't feel right. My therapist and I discussed what I could change. I realized I needed to make some adjustments that would be conducive to me and my healing journey. I had to adjust my surroundings to match a more therapeutic, less distracting environment. I realized that I needed to sit in a completely different room that would allow me to let all distractions fall away and to focus on myself.

We have a guest room where there is a bed, a dresser and a chair that I placed in there for many reasons. I bought this chair when my husband and I decided that we wanted to start a family. At first, it was just a chair that sat in our bedroom by the window, where I would read, relax and dream of our future family. You see, I figured it wouldn't take long for me to get pregnant and I would need a place to sit as I held our baby while it either slept or breastfed. It's a nice chair, one that is stylish, can match any room and reclines easily. The chair has a lot of meaning. It brings up many emotions for me. It brought up so much that I had decided that I needed to move it from our bedroom to the guest room so the reminder it holds would fade over time. I just knew that our guest room, that now was the home to this chair, was the perfect place for my therapy sessions. It would allow me to let go of the resentment I had towards this chair while I grieve my losses. All of the losses that were tied to my Postpartum Depression as well as healing and being grateful for still being alive.

Week after week, I signed on to the portal for my sessions not sure what I would feel, what emotions I would experience and what ah-ha moments I would have. Sitting in that chair with my laptop, I would communicate with my therapist. I felt more and more comfortable as I began to acknowledging my pregnancies, grieving my babies as well as finding hope again in what could be even if I had no idea what my future held. It was hard for me to open up in the beginning, but with time, I knew she was the right therapist for me. At first, we did a lot of art therapy. Even as an artist, I couldn't understand its purpose. Yet, it really allowed my heart to do the speaking.

In June, my therapist informed me that she was graduating from her program and had to move on from her internship. I was heartbroken but this time it was different. She knew that in my past, I had many relationships, including therapeutic ones that ended abruptly. She understood all too well that I had so much loss in my life. She made sure that our time together wouldn't end abruptly but with a sense of closure. Our last appointment fell on July 1. I felt that I had made a lot of progress and knew when our time came to a close, it was what was needed for me to heal even more.

I continued journaling when I felt up to it. Most of the time, I just tried to take care of myself and not feel guilty if I missed a workout. After all, we were still in the midst of the Pandemic. The hardest part during this past year has been seeing all the pregnancy announcements, birth announcements and then hoping that the Pandemic would end so my husband and I could continue our journey of becoming parents. However, with the Pandemic still wreaking havoc on the world and keeping most of us in isolation, I just kept being thankful that we were safe, healthy and together.

Many months passed before my husband found out that a fertility clinic, based out of New York, was going to soon have a location in Colorado that would only be two hours away from us. This was great news! Not only could we switch fertility clinics, but we wouldn't have to travel out of state. The only question, "*Was I ready to continue my journey to motherhood?*" I decided to set up a consultation with the doctor to discuss my infertility history and to really find out if IVF was truly an option for us. I just wanted to know. I wasn't sure if the door was wide open, slightly open or slammed shut. I called the fertility clinic and was able to schedule my consultation for November 2, 2020, at 7 am. Now, I just had to wait for two months without giving up hope.

Finally, my appointment arrived. I was nervous and excited to find out what the possibilities of IVF would be. I signed on to the Zoom call, met the doctor and the health history questions began. As I explained our infertility history, all of it, including the two losses in the last year, my emotions almost got the best of me. As my emotions flooded every ounce, I just apologized to the doctor. He understood and said that he knows what kind of journey it must have been up to this point and that there was no reason that I couldn't do IVF. I was relieved, scared, anxious and excited. Ugh, I felt a huge weight lift off my shoulders while a new hope began to grow in my heart. I thought I had lost all hope. On that day, during my consultation with my new Fertility Doctor, I found it again.

As I sit here and write about my journey over the past few years. It has been one year since my second loss and two years since my first. A year ago, I was hurt, mad and heartbroken. The year prior I also experienced a very similar loss. Both were due to an ectopic pregnancy. A year ago, I was recovering from life-saving emergency surgery where I found out that I was a few months pregnant and I was losing the baby. It was if I was reliving my first loss, but this time it was life-threatening. "How much a difference a year can make?", is an interesting statement. The years 2018 and 2019 were all about loss. Loss I never imagined I would ever experience once, let alone twice. Not only was I grieving from the loss of my two pregnancies, I felt that I lost all hope. Now, a year from my last loss, I have a renewed sense of hope. I am filled with so much emotion as I will be starting IVF on Christmas Eve. I am in awe that after so much loss, I can still hold space for the faith and belief that I may one day become a mom to a child of our own. I know that God has a purpose. Though I may never understand it, I do have to believe that my story of becoming a mom isn't over. Through all of this, I have found hope amongst the loss.

Erin Baer is a thriving entrepreneur and lives her passions as an Author, International Keynote Speaker and Empowerment Coach. Being a survivor of domestic violence and sexual assault, Erin began telling others her story of grace and grit on her road to recovery. This sharing of her personal story became the basis for her book, "From Beaten to Badass". The powerfully worded personal memoir gives readers the strength, hope, and courage to keep going and become the BADASS women they were always meant to be. Erin also founded the organization Beaten to Badass to empower and support those who have been beaten down by life. Her life's work is to enable beaten down and silenced women to once again be strong, courageous, and proud. Erin decided to be the positive voice to show all women that their circumstances don't define them, that they don't need to be beaten down in life, and that they too can be their own heroes. Through her coaching and speaking, Erin encourages you to look within yourself where you will find the power to unleash the badass in you. You may feel defeated and feel life is unfair by the cards you were dealt. However, the only way you lose is if you don't learn and you don't get back up. You are a badass!

CHAPTER 5
JANET

"Life is a mirror and will reflect back to the thinker what he thinks into it." – Ernest Holmes

When I first started looking at myself in mirrors, I was a child delighted with seeing myself. What a strange and wonderous creature I saw looking back at me! I loved the sparkle in my eyes, the way my dimples showed when I smiled, how shiny my hair looked in the light! I could move, sway, dance with myself...it was magical!

Oh, so subtly, when I would catch a glimpse of myself in the mirror, I began to focus on what I didn't see, what wasn't there, how I didn't measure up. I don't know how old I was when I started to criticize what I saw in the mirror. I just stopped being delighted with my own image.

As the years passed and I matured, my criticism of my image in the mirror ran the gamut from one of mild displeasure to outright antagonism. I was too short, too fat, my hair was too straight, I didn't look good in that outfit, my eyebrows were too thick, my hands were ugly, my thighs too big, and on and on and on. I had plenty of mirrors around me lending support and veracity to my self-criticism.

Magazines, newspapers, television and movies had beauty featured by thin women. Growing up, we always watched the Miss America pageant. I can still hear Bert Parks singing, "There she is, Miss America! There she is, your ideal…"

When I had lunch or dinner with women friends and women in my family, we spent a lot of time talking about needing to lose weight, or how "bad" we were if we ordered food that didn't appear to support the current weight loss fad.

I noticed how other women looked in their clothing. If someone looked great, I would tell myself that I couldn't look as good as she did. If someone looked bad in an outfit, I would run a critical message in my head about how she should lose weight. I would look at thin women and think that they must have fast metabolisms, or they starved themselves, or they were unhappy, or they were rich, they probably had a personal trainer and a personal chef, …

Somewhere, amid all those critical thoughts, I also lost the enjoyment of eating. I was not overweight as a child and I have no memory of fighting with food, or that food was "bad". Mealtime came around and we sat down to the table to eat. That was that. As I grew older, I was often the person preparing meals for the family. I never labeled anything I made for a meal as bad food or unhealthy food. Food was part of our day. It wasn't something to dread. We didn't talk about eating or not eating a food in relation to whether we would gain or lose weight. We enjoyed mealtime.

My attitudes around food were much the same when I was raising my children. I prepared similar meals to those I had known and prepared growing up. My battle with food came later.

It is interesting to me that while the food I was eating was the same, my body image changed. For many years, when I looked into the mirror, I told myself I saw a fat person. Today, when I look at pictures of myself during that same time frame, I was not fat. I can't believe I ever thought I was overweight then!

It is not what we say out loud that really determines our lives.
It is what we whisper to ourselves that has the most power.
– Salt Lick Lessons

Remember the scene in *The Wizard of Oz* when the Cowardly Lion is holding his tail with his eyes closed speaking to himself with great emotion, "I do believe in spooks. I do believe in spooks. I do, I do, I do, I do, I do, I do believe in spooks…"? His wanting to be brave while feeling afraid is one of the reasons we love the character of the Cowardly Lion.

Saying out loud that, "I want to lose weight", while at the same time whispering:

"I can't do this",

"This is hard",

"Losing weight is for people with fast metabolisms,"

"I don't want to work out that much",

"I don't want to give up my favorite foods",

"I don't want to be that person at a restaurant who can't eat anything on the menu",

"I'll start a new diet next week, next month",

"Diets don't work anyway", or

"What was I thinking?"

My outer brave has a hard time with my inner fear. My constant whispers to myself are far more powerful and convincing to me than my wishful words.

My battle with my body image and weight creeped into my life unconsciously. Somewhere around the time of my first son's birth, I started to think of my body differently. I had gained a lot of weight during that pregnancy and suffered post-partum depression. I clearly remember sitting on the bed in my mother's bedroom crying because my baby was already two months old and I was still wearing maternity clothes! I had not lost the baby weight.

I started referring to myself as a "beached whale". Although I would laugh when I made this remark, I felt miserable, ugly and incompetent.

About two years later I finally lost the baby weight from my first pregnancy and did not gain as much weight with the next two pregnancies. However, I hung on to the same body image and negative self-talk even when I was slimmer. For most of my adult life, I cultivated thoughts of dissatisfaction with my body. No big surprise then when I became pregnant with my second son, my fourth child. I gained all the same weight as I did with the first child, and again, suffered the same distressing post partem depression and went through the same fight to lose the weight.

My second husband had no tolerance for anyone who carried extra weight. I was slim when we met, and he expected that I would not gain an ounce. He monitored my food, we walked every night and hiked once a week. I watched what I put in my mouth for fear that I would gain weight. Although I enjoyed walking and hiking, there was a lot of stress to never miss an activity that would keep me thin. I was anywhere from a size 2 to a size 6 during those years. What is astonishing to me is, despite hard evidence to the contrary, I still thought of myself as fat.

How often over the years have I heard myself say things like:

"I can't wear that; I would look ridiculous!"

"I inherited my dad's thunder thighs!"

"I look at lettuce and gain five pounds!"

"Can you believe the roll I have around my waist?"

"I don't need a cushion, mine is built in."

"I wouldn't be caught dead wearing that!"

"No matter what I do, I gain weight."

"Food likes me, it hangs on to its favorite places."

My brother-in-law would say, "I'm not overweight, I'm vertically challenged."

I clung to that self-deprecating humor.

I may as well have been saying to myself, "I do believe in fat, I do believe in fat, I do, I do, I do, I do, I do, I do believe in fat."

All those years when I thought I was so overweight, I look back and wish I was that thin again.

Later in my life, I was not only obese, I was terribly ill. When I look at pictures of myself during those years, it is hard for me to understand how anyone (especially me) could have looked at me and seen a healthy person. My face was red and blotchy, my eyes were yellow, my knees and back hurt, and I was out of breath from even the slightest effort. Heartburn, acid reflux, constipation and bloating were my constant companions. I rarely felt good after eating anything. I was suffering from chronic GI (gastrointestinal) problems which was eventually diagnosed as diverticulitis. Some years later, I underwent colon surgery. The emotions of disgust, disappointment and defeat were all wrapped up in my self-talk, too.

"When food becomes the enemy, every time we lose the fight,
we not only gain weight, but lose our self-esteem as well."
– Jane Fonda

My big weight gain started after my children were grown. When my children were at home, I made menus and prepared food routinely. I lost that routine once they were out on their own.

I had no interest in making myself the bad guy in my story of eating. It was so much easier to see anything else, including food, as the enemy. Some of my favorite foods no longer tasted good to me and I decided it was menopause, the stress of my job, the stress of my marriage, part of the aging process, my husband wanted different foods at mealtimes, etc. These things were not the reason food tasted differently to me, but these things were all playing a part in my struggling self-image.

During this time, when I made a salad, it was iceberg lettuce with a few slices of cucumber and maybe a hot house tomato smothered in thousand island dressing. I did not enjoy it. I don't even like iceberg lettuce, but I sentenced myself to this salad regularly. For variety, I would make that same salad with some carrots and possible a little celery.

I would see an article in a magazine about losing weight and try out the diet. I would buy the newest diet craze book and try it. There was the grapefruit diet, the egg diet and the soup diet. I did high protein, low carb, low fat or no fat. I even bought a weight loss franchise. I lost more money than weight!

I remember being hungry all the time and never satisfied with what I ate. Food was no longer enjoyable. When I would eat something I did enjoy, it was usually something sugary or salty, like chips. I would berate myself later for the momentary guilty pleasure.

Rather than buy clothes, I became more interested in buying shoes, scarves, and earrings. I told myself the accessories would add variety to my wardrobe, and I wouldn't be spending as much money on clothes. Never mind that some of the shoes and scarves were just as expensive – or more – than any outfits I purchased.

When I did buy clothing, I started to buy loose fitting clothes. I told myself I was going for a more relaxed casual style. Never mind that I was attracted to more fitted classic clothing, or even somethings with a little drama and flair. I told myself those days were over. I was too old, too over-weight, too timid to wear those kinds of things anymore. I was being practical!

Never mind how I felt. Never mind what I thought... Just never mind!

Going out to eat with my women friends is another experience with that demon, food. Someone will order a creamy pasta dish and then feel bad about herself. She will decide not to have anything to drink or not to have a dessert to "make up" for her bad meal selection. Another will order salad. Then, there's the one who looks longingly at your plate and asks if she can have a little taste of what you're having. Someone else will order something like fried chicken and then proceed to offer up how this is so out of the ordinary and that she is "treating" herself this one time, all the while feeling bad about it. We've all been there. I've been all of these women at different times and places.

I've seen this scene played out many times at family gatherings, at parties with friends. Food is at the center of our social lives. Holidays, work parties, and family celebrations are events with food as a central player. With so many people worried over what they "should" eat, these events hold additional impact and a lot of stress. Even when we let it go and eat what is offered at these gatherings, we very often chastise ourselves for our choices.

My client, Aurora, shared a story with me about her struggle at a party. She had decided to eliminate sugar from her diet. She was having success with her efforts and had started to feel really good about it. Not long into her decision to implement this practice, she was at a luncheon where the group was celebrating a member's birthday. Aurora is a thoughtful, caring, polite woman. She didn't know what to say when she was served a piece of cake, so she accepted the cake. Then she sat at the table trying to think of a way to politely not eat the cake, not have anyone notice that she was not eating the cake and not offend the hostess or the woman whom they were celebrating. Internal knots were forming. Aurora considered hiding the cake in her napkin, but reconsidered as she would have been profoundly embarrassed if someone noticed her hiding the cake. She considered taking it to the lady's room and getting rid of it there but was too afraid someone would see her and didn't want the risk of embarrassment.

When we talked about Aurora's dilemma that day, I asked her if she had considered saying, "No, thank you" when offered the cake. She said she thought that to not accept the cake would be rude and she did not want to be rude.

As we discussed Aurora's choices, it occurred to her that being polite, and being perceived as a polite person, was more important to her than not eating sugar was to her. Although she accepted the piece of cake, she felt awful about it. She felt that she was being "bad". Plus, after having abstained from sugar for a while, when she ate the piece of cake, she immediately had a headache.

Aurora set herself up to feel bad no matter what choice she made that day. Saying no thank you made her feel bad about not being polite. Accepting and eating the cake made her feel bad about not keeping her no sugar commitment to herself. Because Aurora realized that her politeness was a deeply held belief, one she was not ready to change, we talked about how she might be able to accept the cake and feel good about herself.

The cake was offered as a celebration of a woman Aurora admired. So, we can say the cake was offered in love. If it was offered in love, could she eat it in love? If she could eat it in love, can she love herself for participating in this celebration of love? Could she allow herself to feel good about her choice, knowing it was an exception, not a routine? Over time, as she became more confident in her commitment to eliminate sugar, she may be able to say, "No, thank you", when offered a piece of cake and feel good about that choice also.

Just looking at the situation and giving herself permission to have choices and polite ways to implement her choices was freeing for Aurora. Finding a way to feel good about herself whether, or not, she ate the piece of cake was a breakthrough moment. The cake was no longer the demon.

There are over one hundred and fifty diets out there, each promoting the "best" way to lose weight, maintain weight, feel good, etc. No wonder there is confusion! Depending on the last article or book we've read, food takes on new challenges, another sense of what is "bad" for us as fast as diet books are published. We put ourselves at the mercy of expert's opinions of what is good or bad for us.

Making food the bad guy is so easy in today's processed food environment. Most processed food is not as healthy for us as fresh food. Eating a chip or other snack food does not make us bad. Ask yourself truthfully, how do you feel when you eat highly processed food?

There was a time in my life when I was eating so much processed food that I had no idea how I felt, or what I would feel like eating fresh food. Weaning myself from chips, cookies, candies, sodas, breads, boxed and packaged foods is an ongoing process.

 Where are you on the spectrum? Does your food come from the Green Plant or the Cement Plant?

Most of us are eating somewhere in between. The closer our choices are to the green plant, the fresher the food is when we consume it, the higher it is in nutritional density. Also, I discovered, that the fresher choices I make regarding my food, the more energy I have, especially in the afternoon. My traditional 3 o'clock slump doesn't creep up on me when I give my body real food all day long.

> *"All you need is love. But a little chocolate now and then doesn't hurt."*
> *– Charles M. Schulz*

Good job! Have a cookie!

There's treats for good children.

Let's celebrate! I'll get the cake!

Eat all your dinner and you can have dessert.

I can relate to those statements as a child growing up, I've also been the person making those statements. Although we didn't have a lot of sweets in our diet growing up, I still remember thinking of sweets, soda, a slice of pie as a reward. If I did something good, I would be rewarded with something special to eat.

Likewise, my children didn't receive sweets in their diets growing up, yet I continued the tradition of offering food as a reward for good behavior.

My second marriage had a lot of food/love implications. Here I was a grown woman, yet I was terrified to eat food that would add any weight to my body...love would be withheld. I would feel unloved. My self-talk had no words of self-love. Expecting others to provide me the love I sought set me up for an unfulfilling time in my life. Of course, there were many good times during those years, I must admit. However, my internal life was a wasteland of insecurity.

When that marriage ended, I discovered food again. For several years, I was comfortable and slim. Marriage number three catapulted me into obesity. I took my unhappiness out by eating. I was very lonely in this marriage. My children were adults. I found myself lost and food was solace. No one was ever going to tell me what I could or couldn't eat again! So, I ate a lot of food that felt good to me. That turned out to be breads, lots of sauces, meats, fried foods, chips, soda, etc. My third husband suffered with mental illness and the stress of holding everything together took an enormous toll on me. Eating my stress away did not work…that is when diverticulitis entered the picture. I suffered for many years not knowing what was wrong with me. Doctors thought it was female trouble, even though years earlier I had undergone a hysterectomy. Finally, in tremendous pain, I was hospitalized via the emergency room, the diagnosis – diverticulitis. Two years later, I divorced and had colon surgery – both, life changing events!

The surgery gave me a new lease on life. I hadn't felt so good in years! I was living on my own for the first time in my life and it was exhilarating! At first, my children were worried about me living alone. I suppose there were some grounds for their concern. I was the oldest of eight children, had four children of my own, plus I had been married three times. I had people around me all the time for most of my life. What they didn't know I craved, and what I hadn't yet discovered, was how much I would enjoy Freedom! Glorious Freedom!

My post-surgical checkup left me with a clean bill of health. When I asked my doctor about what I could eat, how I should change my diet so that I wouldn't find myself here again, he said I could do whatever I wanted. The surgery was successful, they got everything. I was clean as a whistle!

That made no sense to me. If I went back to eating whatever I wanted, living in a hell hole of stress, I would end up back in the operating room with no additional colon to lose. I would have a bag outside of my body for the rest of my life. No Way! I left his office that day determined to begin a new life in every possible way!

What I learned later was that determination alone does not keep me slim, trim, fit or healthy. Knowing my body, listening to how

I feel when I eat, or don't eat, certain foods allow me the freedom to eat healthfully while enjoying the food and the company with whom I share a meal.

I recognized that I emotionally charge food when I view food as "bad" or not good for me. Taking ownership of how I feel about food and my body has been a good step in the direction of stress-free eating. Finding the good in food and in my body empowers me to make choices that support me in feeling strong and vital. I have days when I just don't want to cook and I'm sick of the whole idea of eating the same food. I've always said that I teach what I need to learn. This has never been more true for me than with food and body image. I am on this journey with my clients and you, dear reader.

Janet Langmeier has worked with organizations and individuals, helping them build their dreams, accelerate their results, and create richer, more fulfilling lives for 30 plus years. A sought-after speaker, teacher, and coach, Janet leads transformational workshops and retreats, group and individual coaching programs, and movement programs.

A Certified Life Mastery Consultant and Transformational Life Coach, Janet's work blends spiritual principles with practical real-world application. She believes in the ability to create mastery in one's world. Her commitment to seeking different perspectives and expanded horizons helps one to push boundaries and delight in unexpected discoveries by embracing a "no limits" philosophy in life.

Chapter 6
SALLY

"Challenges are what make life interesting; over-coming them is what makes life meaningful."
– Joshua J. Marine

It is not enough to just dream or ask for what we want in life. We must be willing to do things differently. Do you remember Einstein's definition of Insanity, "Doing the same thing over and over again and expecting different results?"

The word "Change" is a verb. It requires action in order to achieve.

"INACTION IS A WASTE OF A GOOD RESOURCE – YOU!"

We are all born with our own personal toolbox. That box of strengths and weaknesses that is different for each of us. Some may be the same as others and some are not.

I discovered certain tools I had and what others have, based on life experiences. It is these tools that help me through the challenges in life.

What was your dream in childhood? What did you hope to become? Do you know WHY you wanted to do this? I would bet that when you were dreaming you were not thinking of what challenges you might face while on that journey?

When I was growing up the adults and teachers were always asking these questions. I bet they still are! Teachers are like that.

Do you want to be a Teacher, Nurse, Doctor, Lawyer, Astronaut, Fireman…the list goes on. Nowhere did I ever answer Hairstylist, Insurance Agent or Author! But truthfully, all the skills I learned growing up and all the "tools in my toolbox" came in handy for many different types of work I could have gone into.

Everything happens when it is supposed to based on the decisions we make at different times in our lives. Life is about give and take and the decisions we make every minute of every day. Almost everyone has challenges. Some more than others. It is how you react and move through or around these challenges that has a lasting effect on our lives.

In order for you to grow you have to be open to adjusting as changes come your way. I like to remind myself that the word Change is a verb which means there must be an Action in order for something different to happen.

I grew up in a very loving home. My dad was in the Air Force, my mom was a stay-at-home mom and I have a sister who is 13 months older than me. Being a military family, we lived in many locations. But for us, never out of the United States. Sometimes we lived in a town like Albuquerque, New Mexico and other times we lived on a military base like Vandenberg Air Force Base on the west coast of the US.

I was blessed to live and learn in many wonderful towns across this vast country we call America. My family lived in most every part of it at one time or another. I was born in the state of Michigan, which is surrounded by the Great Lakes. This includes Lake Michigan, Lake Erie, Lake Huron, Lake Superior and Lake Ontario. It is a stunningly beautiful part of the country.

On the east coast we lived in Massachusetts then we moved westward living in Ohio, Michigan, North Dakota, Idaho, New Mexico, Texas, Kansas, and California.

Before I entered 1st grade, we had lived in Michigan, Ohio and Massachusetts and New Mexico. I began 1st grade in Idaho and halfway through the school year my dad was transferred to Texas which is a huge state in the southern part of the country. Each state has its own set of rules for when children can begin 1st grade. Even though I was already halfway through 1st grade the Texas school district would not let me finish. This is one of my earliest remembrances of "unfairness" of the world. Or so my seven year-old self felt. You see, I have a September birthday and for the State of Texas you must be seven years old by the end of August. I had missed their cutoff date.

This had an impact on me at an incredibly early age. The school my sister got to attend had a big yellow school bus that I did not get to ride on! I remember crying and misbehaving because I could not ride on that bus with my sister. I was completely devasted as I thought I was a big girl now going to school and getting to ride on a yellow school bus.

It was one of my earliest lessons on you do not always get what you feel you should. Others will have more control and power. In my case it was the Texas School Board. Because trust me, my mom and dad wanted me in school!

When I was in 4th through 8th, grade we lived in North Dakota. It shares its northern border with the country, Canada, our northern neighbor about 300 miles away. I learned a lot about leadership and standing up to people during this time of my life. Especially adults when they try to compare you with an older sibling. My sister and I are different personalities, and I would say I was a bit more outspoken than my sister. Adults around me gave me many opportunities to step into leadership roles and stretch myself trying new things that were not exactly in my comfort zone. By the time we moved from North Dakota I was helping put together mini-carnivals with games for younger children and bowling on a competitive team.

Because I was an "older" student in the classroom it gave me leadership advantages. To this day, I believe it helped me learn life lessons sooner than those I was in class with. Whenever we moved, we had to meet new people and learn to fit in no matter what the circumstances. You were not guaranteed to be attending school on the military base. When that happens, you must fit in with groups that had been around each other their entire lives. Breaking in was not an easy task. Especially for elementary age children.

Reading people's facial expressions and body language is something I learned early in life and continue to hone over time. By that, I mean watching people's body language for being open or closed to talking with you and the words they used. Were they friendly or not? To this day I can walk into a room and know those who are welcoming and those who are not. But I must always be careful and decide if that person is an extrovert like myself or an introvert. As many introverts are quiet and give off an illusion of being closed. When in fact they are friendly, but only with people they are comfortable and familiar with.

My reason for sharing this bit of background with you is to let you know that no matter what challenges you come up against, you have already learned how to deal with them. You just might not realize it yet!

One of the many challenges I received as an adult was starting a family. Many of you probably have several children and when you decided to do so, everything went just like the books, videos and doctors tell you it will. That is what I thought my story would be as well. Surprise! That was not my story. I know it was not the story for many of you.

Not all couples get married and have children right away. My husband and I had been married for 10 years when we decided we were finally settled enough to start a family.

Right before my husband, Paul, and I we were married, he was attending Cal Poly University in San Luis Obispo, California, USA. For those of you who do not know, California is on the West Coast of the United States. We spent two and a half years there. I was a cosmetologist at the time specializing in haircutting.

We loved San Luis Obispo and if Paul could have found a job in his field we would still be living there. It is a beautiful, quaint college town with a personality all its own.

Once Paul graduated, he accepted a job with a large financial services company. At first, they were going to move us to Tarzana, CA which is just outside Los Angeles, CA. Instead, we were in Santa Barbara, CA. Again, challenges abounded with the limbo you can find yourself when a company cannot make up its mind where to move you.

Santa Barbara is a beautiful city nestled between the foothills of the Santa Ynez Mountain range which is a part of the Los Padres National Forest. We were fortunate to live there for four and half years. The Pacific Ocean was less than 10 minutes from our home and that was only because there were stoplights to wait for.

The problem with Santa Barbara at the time was they still had restrictions on places to live. For example, our housing complex did not allow children to live there. It was an Adult Only complex. When we started looking for a home or condominium, they were awfully expensive and many communities did not allow for children or you had to be 55 years of age or more to live there. We did not have any children, but we certainly thought we would at some future date.

After four and a half years, his company moved us to Eugene, Oregon. We went from 300 plus days of beach sunshine to 300 days of rain and clouds. It was a difficult adjustment, but adjust we did.

The great part of the move was we were able to purchase a home. In Santa Barbara homes were out of our reach financially. For those of you not familiar the State of Oregon is directly north of the state of California. Eugene, Oregon was 16 hours north of Santa Barbara, California.

We both went to work. My husband continued to do what he had always done within the financial services industry, but with new people and a new office. I was still a cosmetologist and had to get relicensed for Oregon. But once I did, I went to work at a salon styling hair and learning to live with humidity and cloudy days.

After four years, we decided that we had a home, we both had good jobs we were settled into our routine. Perhaps it was time to start a family? We both thought two children would be perfect.

I grew up with a sister who is 13 months older than myself and my husband had an older brother and three younger sisters. So, neither of us had huge families. Two children would be perfect and if we were lucky, we would have one boy and one girl.

Thankfully, we got pregnant soon after we made our minds up that we were ready. When you tell the universe what you want, you had better be ready when it delivers as we were expecting soon after the decision was made.

My husband was at an advanced school for his job in June for three weeks and when we talked on the phone, I told him that next year he would be able to celebrate Father's Day, finally. He was quiet for a moment, then it dawned on him what I was saying.

Our baby's due date was determined to be February 15th. Everything was going smoothly. I was not sick once in those early days and believe me I heard all the morning sickness stories and was thankful it was not part of my journey.

However, I might have taken on morning sickness rather than what we had to go through the last trimester. It was two weeks before Thanksgiving which is a busy time for hairdressers because my clients all wanted to look good for the holidays. I was completely booked through the Christmas and New Year's holidays.

I went to my regularly scheduled doctors' visits. His nurse, Shirley, was a tough one. I always thought of her as a no-nonsense drill sergeant. She had a gruff voice that would scare anyone. She came in and was checking my heartrate and blood pressure. She looked a little funny and took my blood pressure a second time. She was not happy, and when Shirley is not happy that is a serious problem. She asked me what I had been doing that day and I told her I had been working up until it was time for my appointment.

She told me my blood pressure was elevated. She gave me a blanket and pillow, shut off the light in the exam room and asked me to rest and relax and she would be back in 30 minutes. I did not think anything of it, as all of this was new to me. I am a healthy person and not on any medications.

Thirty minutes goes by and she comes back in and my blood pressure had not come down. My doctor also was there, and it was determined that an ultrasound was needed to see if the baby was doing okay. The heartbeat had been okay.

The ultrasound was fine, but they determined that I was to be put on bed rest from that day forward. In addition, I was put on blood pressure reducing medicine and an anti-seizure drug. My blood pressure was so high, they thought I would have a stroke.

Quickly several thoughts started running through my head. You know those things you THOUGHT were important, but in reality, you just needed to take a pause and reflect on what truck just hit you!

My first thought was all my clients for the next six weeks were going to have to go to someone else. I would lose all that income. I worked on commission so if I was not seeing clients, I made no money. No such thing as vacation pay or paid sick days in my industry at the time.

Bed rest it was. The instructions given to me were that I could be up for 20 minutes every hour. Otherwise, I was to be laying down. My doctor appointments were every three days because I was now considered High Risk.

Every single appointment was important to keep us both on the right track. Although, truth be known, those first few weeks in January I was getting tired of every three days of doctor appointments.

Even though the drive to the doctor's office was not a great distance, the city of Eugene had a horrible parking problem. It was always a struggle to find a parking space and quite honestly at this juncture, an aggravation.

Obviously, my mental state was losing patience. Not for the doctors or our baby. This was my first real "adult" dealing with a situation that I was unable to control. Anyone who knows me understands control is how I live my life. I live a well-balanced and fully involved life. Which means that being told I must stay laying down 40 minutes out of every hour did not fit in with my control. I was an active person and not used to being home all day, every day. All my friends were working.

Right after Christmas, they began doing ultrasounds every other appointment. At one of these appointments, it was determined that our baby was sitting feet first. They had already determined I would be delivering before the February 15th due date. This was not going to work.

They tried many different options to get the baby to change positions, but none worked. Mostly because I had developed a benign tumor the size of a grapefruit which left no room for movement. We would just have to work with feet first.

Our next appointment was on the afternoon of Monday, January 14th. My husband attended all the appointments once I was diagnosed as high risk as we seemed to have a surprise at each visit. Another new twist or turn to change our lives around.

We did not understand at the time, but it was the Universe's humor in teaching us to be flexible and forget setting expectations that can change quickly. This lesson was another "tool" for my toolbox which has served me well over the years. Expect the unexpected and be resilient, which means being able to withstand and change quickly.

We went in as we always did. Blood pressure check and an ultrasound were on the docket for that day. They wanted to see how the baby was developing and an ultrasound was the best way.

The ultrasound technician came in and started her procedures. After a couple of tries, she stepped out of the room and came back a few minutes later with our physician. She reran the ultrasound. Our baby's heartbeat would be fine, then it would drop to almost a flat line, then slowly climb back up to normal. Only to quickly sink again.

Our physician made his decision quickly. The next thing I knew, we were on our way to the hospital for an emergency Caesarean Section. Which means they were going to perform surgery to deliver our baby THAT DAY!

On our drive over to the hospital, we were going through the lists of things to do that we were not prepared for. Top of the list was for my husband to call our neighbor and good friend to make sure our cat was fed and to let her know that we would have a baby in less than an hour.

Once we arrived on the maternity floor of Sacred Heart Hospital, things moved very quickly. The nurse putting my IV line in was so nervous she missed the vein in my hand. If you could see my veins, they are huge and difficult to miss. But miss them she did. My doctor happened to walk in at that moment and ask the nurse to leave and send in her supervisor, who then put the IV in with no issue. You see, not only was our baby struggling to breathe, but my blood pressure was off the charts. They wanted to run the same tests at the hospital as they did in his office to make sure it was not an issue with their equipment. It was quickly decided that the baby was under major distress and needed to be delivered immediately! Also, my blood pressure was rising, and they needed to keep me from having a stroke.

My husband returned to the room that was pure chaos. He was told I was being prepped for emergency surgery.

He went white and the nurse asked him if he was okay. He was a bit in shock as he did not expect that. The nurse told him that if he passed out, they would simply move him to the side and step over him as the baby and I were the priority.

Within a few minutes we were in surgery.

Our daughter, Meredith, was delivered at 6:18 pm on Monday, January 14th. She was quickly taken to a heated isolette in the room and then wheeled directly to the Neonatal Intensive Care Unit, fondly referred to as the NICU. The NICU pediatricians and staff worked on getting her cleaned up and keeping her warm. The staff made sure she had 10 fingers and 10 toes. They also weighed and measured her. They gave her oxygen and set up an IV on her as well. Her heartrate became stable once she was delivered and put on oxygen. She was delivered 3 weeks early. She weighed in at a whopping 3 lbs. 8 oz and was 17 inches long. We had ourselves a petite baby girl. She fit all the categories for a premature baby. She was delivered under a high-risk pregnancy, delivered by caesarean section with a complicated delivery as I was a stroke risk.

My physician continued to take care of me and once he and his team were done, I was wheeled into the NICU to see our daughter. She was in a completely enclosed, heated isolette. The only way to get to her was through arm holes in the sides of the unit. They had her all hooked up to monitors and oxygen. After a few minutes, I was taken back to my room.

The maternity ward is a noisy place. There are babies crying up and down the hallway. Most moms can have their babies in their rooms, which is why it was no noisy. I was angry that I could not have my daughter with me. I had to be wheeled down to the NICU. Once there, we had to scrub with betadine soap and make sure we were as sterilized as we could be before entering the area where the babies were kept.

Anger is a feeling that many of us have when we are not in control of a situation or challenge. You must allow yourself, within reason, to work through this anger as it is just as much a part of you as happiness. It is a time for introspection about why we are angry. There is always a part of you that asks, "why me? What did 'I' do to deserve this?" It is part of our self-preservation and protection from the outside world. I spent quite a bit of time with my anger. I was upset that I became ill and didn't make the extra money at the end of the year. I was angry that I had to have major surgery. I was angry that my baby was struggling to live and other mothers had babies that didn't have to struggle. But in the end of what I like to refer to as my "personal pity party", I understood that I would never be given something I could not work through. My "lesson" was that we are not always in control and stuff happens all the time. Some good and some bad. Bottom line is I was okay and our baby was okay. Do not ask for trouble that hasn't shown up yet at your doorstep.

At the time Meredith was in the NICU there were 20 other babies as well. Sacred Heart Hospital was a regional hospital so babies needing intensive care were all brought here. There were two sets of triplets and three sets of twins joining the group of babies. Meredith, at 3 lbs. 8 oz, was not the smallest by any means.

I must be honest, after spending time in the NICU and then walking by the regular baby nursery was interesting. The regular baby nursery always had the newborns on display so families could see them from a distance. These babies looked so huge! Seeing a regular size newborn weighing in at 8-12 lbs. compared to the NICU where the average weight is around 2-3 lbs. is a huge difference.

I was released from the hospital on day four and went home without Meredith. Which was certainly not what I planned for when we got pregnant.

Meredith was in the Neonatal Intensive Care Unit (NICU) for a total of two weeks. This is much shorter than most NICU babies. Typically, they keep them until they reach the weight, they figured they would be at full term. For Meredith, that would have been 5-6 lbs.

We had no family in Oregon, so there were no worries about family members wanting to see her. My mom and dad lived in California and my in-laws lived in Iowa. My mom suffered a massive heart attack two weeks before Meredith was born and my mother-in-law fell in December and had surgery to put seven metal pins in her leg to keep the bones together. We would have no help running to our rescue.

This meant that we brought her home at 3 lbs. 8 oz. We were strongly urged to not take her out in public and not allow anyone into our home.

I had already been bed ridden almost two months and I was a bit stir crazy with my own company. We did not have the internet, cell phones or cable television. The doctors explained that 80% of intensive care babies were hospitalized a second time during their first 12 months. They were simply susceptible to other germs. They recommended keeping her at home unless for a doctor's appointment her first year.

They set up her well care visits, which were just as awful as my every 3-day visits before she was born! We met her pediatrician an hour before they started seeing other patients in the morning. That way, there were fewer possible germs that could infect her. Also, many people have not seen or held a baby so small, going in early kept us away from those who would be curious.

Because she was so small, regular cloth baby diapers were too big for her. In came another challenge. We had to make arrangements with a company called Pampers and order preemie diapers by the case to be delivered.

Meredith also had digestive issues so she could not easily digest her food. She would cry and writhe and scream in pain from the food fermenting in her poor tummy. This led us to a pre-digested formula for her which was difficult to find and very expensive. We had to search and ask a lot of questions about how to "solve" these issues.

Once this mountain was climbed, she began to grow and thrive. She had and has a fighter personality which is why she survived all the setbacks beginning before she was born.

We are all born with our own personal toolbox. That box of strengths and weaknesses that is different for each of us. Some may be the same as others and some are not.

I discovered certain tools I had and what others have, based on life experiences.

We were living in Eugene, OR where it rains continuously for nine months out of the year. In fact, over 50 inches a year.

It was an especially cold and dismal day and the rain was pouring down as hard as you can imagine. Water running down the street was creating its own fast flowing river. If I were to put a toy sailboat in it, it would be at the end of the block in no time.

I drove a two door, Oldsmobile that had a bench seat in front. Not like today's cars where we have those awesome captains' seats and a button to move our seats forwards and back. Mine was non-electric which meant I would have to manually push it forward to get into the back seat.

Getting Meredith in and out of the car was a chore. I had to push the entire bench seat forward and climb into the back seat to latch and unlatch her from the rear facing car seat.

Whenever I wanted to go somewhere there was a process of several steps. Let me set up the scene for you. When leaving our home our car was in the garage, I would have to push the front seat forward and climb in the back seat with my newborn. After locking her in, I would have to climb back out, pull the front seat back and get in. I would then have to manually open the garage door before getting in to drive.

Now, remember, I was living in rainy Oregon at the time. Once I backed my car out of the garage, I would have to step out of the car in the pouring rain to manually close and lock the garage door.

Coming home from a trip was just a repeat of leaving. It meant I had to get out of my car, manually unlock and open the garage door, climb back into the car, pull it into the garage, get out to manually close the garage door and get then Meredith out of the backseat car seat.

It was quickly determined I needed 2 things:

- A garage door opener
- A new four door car

Buying and installing the garage door opener was the easiest of the two tasks and didn't really cost a lot of money nor much planning was needed.

We went to the hardware store picked it up and had our neighbor, Hank help us install it. Hank worked for a construction company and loved to help his neighbors that were as "handy" with tools and household installations as he was.

On a side note, did you know that garage door openers can come with a set code that you should reset once you have installed it? We did not know this. We found out later that a neighbor up the street from us thought he had an intruder. His garage door kept going up and down and up and down. After my husband and Hank completed the installation, they kept admiring their work by opening and closing the garage door opener. We all had a great laugh over that. Since that day, we have always immediately changed the codes on our garage door openers.

Finding a new car, on the other hand, did take time. I needed to decide what I liked about my current car and what other needs and wants I had.

What I knew was my current 1972 Oldsmobile Cutlass had a lot of power and I like a car that will move. The new car had to have a powerful, strong engine. The second item on my have to list was the new car had to be a 4 door. Those were the must haves.

But with all things in life there are always things we WANT vs NEED. I wanted a car with electronic door locks and seats, a sunroof, air conditioning and cruise control. None of these items were standard in 1985.

In my earlier book titled, "Succeed With Purpose", I share in Chapter 3 – Prepare with Purpose information relating to "knowing your numbers". It talks about knowing where you are financially before you do anything. Which is exactly the tools I used when faced with needing a new car and garage door opener.

Once I had my list made, I had to begin the process of visiting car lots and test driving. Back then, we did not have Car Brokers or Internet! Once I decided on a 1987 Nissan Maxima we sat down and figured out the cost for the car and insurance.

TOOLBOX LESSONS LEARNED: Always know your personal finances (your numbers), not necessarily what you HAVE but how MUCH you need.

- I was asked to quit my career 2 months sooner than I had originally planned. Which meant, no income for me.
- We had to purchase preemie diapers and special food
- I needed to figure out how much money I needed for my new car payment, taxes, licensing and insurance.
- In order to purchase this vehicle, I would need to make some changes. It was decided that I would go back to

work 2 nights a week and that would cover the costs for this new car!

- I was able to quickly figure out if I could afford my car because I knew how much we had in savings and how much my part time job paid. The car would fit because I would add one more day of work.

Finally, it was a cold, rainy and dreary day in Eugene, OR. We had just arrived home after a trip to the store. We pulled up to our home, I pushed the new device on my new car's visor. The garage door lifts gently into the air and I pull my car inside.

Because of the convenience of a garage door opener and a four-door car, my life became easier.

My daughter's safety while riding in the back seat became better (I was able to reach her more easily in an emergency).

My new car was not a hardship as I had figured out a way to pay for it. I had accepted those challenges and found a way to resolve them.

CHANGE IS A VERB....IT TAKES ACTION

It is always my goal to help others figure ways to resolve the challenges that they face in life. Each of us can have the same challenge but go about solving it in different ways. Mostly, based on how we resolved similar ones in our past and on where we are at in life.

For me, I had the money to purchase a new garage door opener but not a new car. It became a game of what car, who to purchase it from, where to purchase it from and when. The major piece was how to find the money to pay for it.

My final thoughts are:

- Children don't arrive with an owner's manual it is a learn as you go training
- How do you make the best of a bad situation?
- Having the wisdom to figure out what is truly important in life
- Remember you can only choose your reactions, not the situations
- Filter advice, while trusting that you understand what works for you
- Learn to break down any goal into bite size pieces

What fills your toolbox? Are you a person who flies by the seat of your pants or someone who needs a play-by-play detailed plan before you can act?

Sally Wurr is a lifelong entrepreneur. She is known as the "storm whisperer" and has an uncanny way of sharing what she has learned in life. Sally is the President and Founder of SW Insurance Corp and served in many leadership roles with non-profit organizations. Her first book, "Succeed With Purpose" was published in 2019 and is available in paperback and Kindle.

CHAPTER 7
SUSIE

Latina Finding Her Right Pair of Shoes

Present time:

I am living the best time of my existence and I'm enjoying every minute of it. Finding the right shoes for the right moment. Life is marvelous. I am sitting here in my living room, cozy with my puffy blanket, watching a Christmas movie as I drink a hot cup of tea, reflecting on where I am and the long road I have traveled to get here. Currently, I have a roof above my head. My two *hijos* are literally young adults, strong, intelligent, compassionate. I have been a proud single mom for over ten years. It seems forever, but it has definitely been a transformative journey for the three of us. After getting divorced, I pursued my Master's Degree. It was easier to picture myself reaching higher goals without the chains of fear and confusion.

It is a true honor to have been an elementary educator for the last nineteen years. Oh Lord, I have seen all kinds of little souls parading through my classroom. Our classroom, where everyone is the teacher for all and the learner of all. The place where I mirror my little self. That's right, reflecting on what my life has been, I have taken the trip in time on several occasions. It is inevitable, my students remind me of how I started my journey to become a self-empowered LATINA. The many obstacles and setbacks, I had to face with the sole determination in mind of SUCCEEDING. Who would even think or consider even the possibility for a little girl from a little *Rancho* in Gunajuato, México, could come this far as a single-mom, to be a teacher, a business woman, an international transformational speaker and a published author, in a foreign country; in a foreign culture, using a foreign language, in a totally new world?

La pequeña niña:

Years ago, in December of 1993 to be exact, sitting on a bench by the front door of my home in México, I contemplated that which was my home, as my identity. Every morning since I turned twelve, I got up early to get ready for work. My favorite task was to harvest cucumbers. "*Vamonos*," my aunts, uncles and friends scream as they wait for me by the gate. "*Mamí ya me voy*," I tell my mamí with an excitement in my heart. A day full of joy, laughs, food, nature, *barro*, a day of dream big way beyond the unknown waiting for me. That smell of wet land, moist soil, the aroma of the green cucumber plant covering my whole glove green -- the color of hope. The endless view of the *surcos*, so long that it almost seems I will find myself in a totally different galaxy when getting to the end. My lungs refuel with fresh clean air, literally touching my soul through my five senses. My genuity revives and reminds me of my true *SER*. How did I ever get lost? *No lo se.*

Summer in the fields is like heaven. It is like having a continuous chance to stop and listen. Somehow that was lost along the way. But oh well, back to that summer. Cropping cucumbers is not the easiest job necessarily. Starting at five am till three or four in the evening, many *campesinos,* myself included, get ready to embark on the trip to their job site, the fields. My dad is in the United States working hard to provide us with a better life, to put food on our table. But apparently there were not enough *dolares.* My mom, two younger brothers and I barely have money to get food on our table or clothes to wear. We are lucky enough to have two rooms, one where my parents and two brothers sleep and the other one, my bedroom which we use as a kitchen too. What can I say? I am the only *chica* in the family, so I get to have my own bedroom. Sometimes I wonder, what is EL *NORTE* like? That *norte* that everybody in my town talks about. That magical money machine, at least that is what many say. What would I do there? Would I finally accomplish my dreams of becoming a singer, an actress, or a teacher? Am I ready to go to that place where dreams come true? I don't know, there has always been a whisper telling me there is more out there than just becoming a *sumisa* wife and mother like every woman, when I grow up. Or is the TV which has shown me that big dreamers do not exist, a lie? I don't think so. Deep inside me there is something that tells me the world of dreams is bigger than what my imagination could ever reach, definitely bigger than my small town.

Lunch in the fields… yummy, but my *tias'* food is the best especially when I am starving after putting my physical body through strenuous stress working all morning long. We all share a little bit of our packed lunches. My *tio* has that unique way of creating a community among strangers who later become family. We have *tortillas recién* hechas enchiladas, fried beans, papas con chile. My *mami* packed me some huevo con chile, eggs with chilli, however I prefer my *tías' tortillas enchiladas*, oh cielos ¡qué delicia! You know it's not necessarily about the food, it is about unity, respect not only towards everyone else, but to ourselves. An experience like this pushed me to value the simple things in life. A laugh, a taco, some quality time, and let the rest of insignificant events roll over happiness. I want that for my whole life.

By the end of the *jornada* of harvesting, my feet are sore from walking in the mud carrying a huge *costal*, a sack full of cucumbers all day long, which wake me up *en el rancho*. When is the day going to be over? I wonder, as the thorns of the cucumber plant go through my gloves and poke my hand. In the meantime, I also imagine a delicious bowl with chili, lime juice and salt where I can dip my baby peeled cucumbers and just have that irresistible taste in my *paladar*, sensational. The perfect way to end a long-drawn-out day in the fields of Guanajuato.

Exhausted of bending my back all day long, my mind can only think of one thing, going to *el norte*, the land of opportunity for a better life, that is what everyone assumes, that is exactly what everybody talks about, that is precisely what I imagined. The absence of shoes to wear is not of a big deal when you have hope, faith and big dreams. When my heart has grown to be strong and determined, at such a young age, it is almost inexplicable, how this little warrior who knows herself very well gets lost in the madness of fake reality. Thank you, mom, for teaching me that women can also be and do whatever they put their mind to.

Finally Heading to "El Norte"
The day finally arrived, we are going to the United States, we are moving to Colorado. Although I am really excited about what

this different world might bring to our lives, I do not necessarily appreciate the date my dad chooses to travel, CHRISTMAS DAY, December 25th, … *¿En serio?* During the best time of the year. When the spirit of love and family and friends getting together is the main ingredient. The holidays that I enjoy the most???? *No jegue vale*!!!! That does not make me happy at all, besides leaving my identity behind, my family, my friends, my culture, we are heading to *"El Norte"* on *el dia de navidad. Pero bueno, donde manda capitán no gobierna marinero,* in other words I could not say no to my father who had sacrificed so much to make this happen, to get all the family to a place where we can have a better life together.

How was it over twenty years ago that I migrated to the United States? As we embark on this family adventure with my dad, whom I love and always says, don't be scared of the unknown. But excited to write yet a better story. The bus took us further than we have even gone before. Enormous wide freeways which seemed endless like my eagerness to pursue my desires … Freeways with all kinds of shapes and directions, almost like a metaphor of the vast options life offers us. I am ready to take them all. Oh yes, I am. Incredible cities. Already different food and language as we are heading more towards the north of the country. Amazing variety of nature views as we went from central to north of Mexico. What happened to the flowers and green trees? I can say now, that I traveled across the country of México, sure!

We are all exhausted, it's been over twenty-four hours since we left Guanajuato. As we crossed the border, I don't know about my two brothers and my parents, but this *chica* is already feeling powerful. I can finally go find my shoes. I can finally accomplish my dreams of being a singer or a computer programmer, or a teacher. Dreams that I have had since I was a little girl, when I was still connected to my inner self.

Oh *cielos*! I am a fifteen-year-old extremely energetic chica, I mean, energetic. I am like the little squirrels you know, running from one place to another back and forth greeting everyone all day long. Doing sports, visiting friends, eating some *sabritas* and candy, running to my *tio Jose's* store to get some bread for dinner, and still have energy to hold a hilarious family gathering with my parents and two brothers. Here, in Colorado, I have to stay inside, confined in our apartment complex. Pulling my hair as I look through the window of my room to what seems to be dead trees, oh my gosh, no colors but gray. See, back in the fields the four seasons' changes are not as noticeable. It is warm all year long. It is green and the roses bloom even in winter time. On the other hand, Colorado has tremendous snow storms and only a month or so of summer, well what can I expect it's the early 90's.

High School
Snow was not the biggest shock. Later, I had to attend a high school that is as big as my town, without friends, and knowing only how to say coffee and donuts in English, thanks to "*La India Maria*" movie. Being fifteen and leaving everything behind, was not easy. What to do now? Going through a grief process was painful. Life was apparently preparing me for what was to come by having me learn and practice some resiliency techniques, already. I am determined to do the best of this situation, I am already feeling the toughness of life transformation, there is no way back just surrender, I do not desire to go back and let go of the lady I am dreaming of and now becoming.

Cultural Shock

It is already January 1994 and I still have no friends. The weather is not as promising either. A cold that penetrates to the bone makes this experience hard as ice. I miss the smell of the wet soil after it rains, the smell of hand-made tortillas on the *comal*, and more than anything, I miss the identity life had shown me until then. It is like something in me is dying. My brothers seem to adapt a little bit faster than me. They already made lots of friends. Hopefully, I can find some when we start to go to school.

We reside in the south part of the city, children attending high school or a grade below, belong to Longs Peak elementary and I was supposed to go to Niwot High School. Instead, I am sent to Skyline High School, which according to the district, has a better system to deal with "newcomers," like me, who speak zero *ingles*. How could no one warn me of the differences among my Mexico and this new place? What a shock, nothing is the same. First day of school becomes a confusing adventure. Here students have lunch provided by the school. Not in my *rancho*. Here students have options on what they want to have for lunch, at least for high schoolers. In my rancho, my mom sent us with a torta and organic orange juice. Here students have so many teachers, how could I remember all their names and their classrooms? Moreover, *no entiendo nada*! I do not understand anything they are saying.

It is very surprising to me to find some people from Guanajuato on the first day of school. As far as I know, during this time in Colorado there were very few Latinos or people who spoke Spanish. In fact, I later learned that my family and I are part of the migration Latino history of Longmont, how cool that is! We became part of the first generation of Latino families in this part of Colorado.

Back to high school now, being laughed at during my history class, where I do not learn anything. I am the only Spanish speaker without any kind of language support and a teacher that does not even bother because he does not know how to connect with me. Learning to say the word "sheet" definitely marked my life forever. Back in my rancho, whenever a U.S citizen visits, we receive her/him with all of our love. Almost the most important visitors of all. I remember one of my *tias* got married to Eric, "*el gringo*" (green go), *oh cielos*. The whole town gathered in a feast to welcome him. He was white after all, right? I don't know, this has always created confusion to me. See, I am *trigeñita, morenita,* brown skin, but beautiful. How come here in Colorado, they did not greet me the same way we greeted *el gringo*? Additionally, can someone explain to me why my own people have rejected me because of my skin color? Life mysteries which continue to train me spiritually and mentally to what it takes to become the lady I visualize to become. On a side note, for years, it has been really hard to say the word sheet and couple others just in case I might not deliver the message I want, you know and pronounce the inappropriate words instead, *que pena,* what a humiliation.

I have been crying for close to two years now, yearning my life back *en el rancho,* my best friend, my family, my culture, my freedom, myself. My family and I go back every two years, it is not the same any more. Something changed inside me, I am another person. Moreover, I cannot go back before I accomplish my dreams. I hear that little voice which is always with me encouraging me to continue regardless of the suffering. My high school counselors talk about pursuing college, a career. I must push a little more, I am almost there, I tell myself as I imagine earning a college degree as a computer programmer. Nevertheless, I don't really know how to navigate the education system here or elsewhere.

Who do I talk to in this poor limited English? How am I going to pay my tuition? Transportation? Lunch? Perhaps this was not for people like me, a Latina, woman of color coming from extreme poverty. *Oh cielos*, this is harder than I ever thought, at least that is what it seems like so far. Where is that little resilient girl from *el rancho*? Where are my shoes? How do I find them now?

I am the first Latina to graduate from Niwot High School, 1996. I feel so proud of myself. A little lost as to not have attended prom, I mean what prom? What do you do in prom? Where is it? No one explained to me what it is. I have no idea. I do not know much English, but my desire to continue in the effort to overtake any cultural and language obstacles is stronger. The new school year started, my friend, Rosi, and I decided to start at a community college. Both of us are very young and naive. Somehow, I start to recognize the leader in me as I see others obtaining a higher education, and even though these are my white classmates, I have a feeling that I will succeed too. I have no idea how, but I will.

Marriage:
A little while after I started college, I decided to get married to my boyfriend of three years. This was *Cielos Santos*, a completely unknown world for me. Not only because it is a marriage, but because of the huge bridge between our perspectives regarding a family. Many red flags have been shown to me that this is not the best freeway of my life, but I ignore them. A Latina woman expected to get married as soon as possible. That means young, like in my 20s. The noise louder than my inner voice. I left school and my dreams with the sole disposition of giving my best to my new family, my husband and son. I left me out. A few years into the marriage, unexpected events begin to happen. Am I being punished for not listening to that whispery voice?

It is a sunny, clear, blue-sky day in April, 2002. By now, I have been blessed with the most precious love of all, my eight-month-old baby boy. Let me tell you a little bit about my first pregnancy. At 23 I got pregnant with my first *hijo*, Richy I love you *amorcito*. During this whole time, I have been hospitalized countless times due to a diagnosis of Ulcers Colitis, a very debilitating disease which has no cure, at least that is what the doctors made believe. My marriage has not been easy, and my physical body has been talking to me through physical illness that this extraneous emotional and mental stress should not be part of us. That I must stop pleasing others by sacrificing my authentic self. Am I paying attention to all these messages and signs? NO!!! I'm in my fifth month of pregnancy or so, when the gastroenterologist warns me of my situation. I have two options, he says, one is to continue with this pregnancy and risk my life or literally kill my baby. I want to cry out loud right now, not possible in a relationship where emotions have been suppressed, so I ingest it all for the … hundredth thousandth time? I do not know, I lost count. If there is one thing that never abandoned me was HOPE. Growing up in that slightly small town was to be resilient, and part of being resilient is having hope for the best. So, my husband at the time and I decided I am going back to Mexico to have a second opinion. So, I did. It was not easy at all, but more than worth it. My son, (now sons), are young adults now, strong and healthy.

Going back to that Friday in April of 2002. That gorgeous bright day was the most obscure day of my life. After having physical therapy to treat an underarm pain, I am sent to my primary physician by my physical therapist. She ordered some x-rays, nothing to be alarmed of, right? Then she suggested having a deeper body scan just to make sure of what? At that point I couldn't imagine the avalanche of cold-freezing news to come. I am starting to worry. But my faith is stronger. Subsequently, after having my CAT scan done, I am sent to a doctor on the third floor, he will talk to me about the results of the procedure. I am alone, confused, lonely, empty. Just thinking how upset my partner will be when he hears the new news. I have nobody to call. I have been separated from my family and friends, I permitted it without noticing. This looks like a *callejon sin salida* a blind alley, with all the doors open.

There is this frightened little girl waiting on some white gown men to tell her who knows what. The doctor walks into this tiny dark room where my x-rays and scans are brightly displaying. A nurse is with him. I am by myself. My stomach was empty, lunch hour had already passed. I had called my job as a teacher assistant, which I started four months ago, I am being held at the clinic. My mind is blank. The doctor starts his diagnosis. "Stage 4 cancer," I heard him saying. Time stopped at that very moment while the doctor continues on pointing to what the images of my scans are showing where the cancer is located in my body. My whole world shatters, but no tears come out of my eyes. I have suppressed these for a long time now to avoid *burlas y humillaciones* at my home. "You have a biopsy on Monday and an appointment with Dr. Johnson, a cancer specialist, who will treat you after we find out if it is a malign or benign type of cancer. As I drive back home, my entire life goes through my mind. There was again that little strenuous voice talking to me and I again did not listen. After six months of torturable chemotherapy and roller coaster emotions as well as physical instability, *la batalla termino*, I have defeated that thing called cancer. How do I do it within a mist of emotional abuse? There is only one answer to that, the resilience techniques that life experience have been giving me have well prepared me to face just any distress. I made a definite decision; I am going to be cancer free for the rest of my life. I am the queen of my fate. But she still has hope for her family to be together as the "normal" family that society and traditions dictate to be. There is hope, my husband finally shows some love towards me and our son.

That little girl from *el rancho* is finding her way back to leave behind so much hate, distrust, loveless miserable marriage life. I started reading all kinds of books on healthy marriages, healthy parents-sons/daughters relationships and many more topics. My mindset is starting to shift. I am no longer here; I am there in that harmonious life I want for my kids and me. After a few years of remission, I decided to have another baby. Originally, I wanted to have four children, then I decided two are good so they can have each other. So, I got pregnant with the most *cachetoncito* baby ever. Favian is born after a magical pregnancy. No complications, everything is just great. Simultaneously, I have taken the opportunity to pursue a Bachelor's degree in public education. During this time, I am taking my newborn to university classes with me. He is now the official university baby; all my classmates love him and help me nurture him. Moreover, I am so thrilled after this long journey full of thorns, to bring my little resilient girl out to life. That's right, I have the determination to overtake any obstacle and make it a milestone to reach my dreams, not only for me, but now I have a bigger reason, my two sons, the loves of my life. My reason to come out of the ashes stronger than ever. My desire to give them a way better *hogar. ¡Si señor!*

The Definite Breakthrough

¡Esto si que no me lo esperaba! I was not expecting this! On December 19th, 2006 I had a routinary procedure scheduled at 8:00am to check my large intestine. I have had a colonoscopy

yearly since I was first diagnosed with ulcer colitis at eighteen, just to make sure that no colon cancer is developing. Surprisingly, it is a glaring December morning. I am actually looking forward to having this exam done. Obviously, I will get some cocktails that will make me forget about my current reality, I definitely need time to myself. Oh boy, I can't even recall the last time I had time on my own, no wonder *por que estoy tan perdida.*

Christmas time, my favorite holiday of the year are just days ahead. I am on my break from college until January when I will start my second semester. Therefore, my children and I already made plans to celebrate as a happy joyful family, only the three of us. Their dad is leaving for Mexico at dawn. We are closer to our freedom, I cheer myself up as I go through glory and hell while being a full-time mom, student, spouse, teacher assistant, and all of the other titles I carry (daughter, cousin, etc). It seems like too much, however the excitement of proving myself that I can attain anything I set my mind to, is greater. I just keep *pedaleando* as far as I can go. The decision has been made and it is definite.

To have a colonoscopy done, an IV is needed, I had to be out so I don't feel any pain as the miniature camera and twisters go inside my large intestine collecting specimens to be examined in a lab. Laying on my left side, I am facing the monitor which displays part of what is going on in my system. At some point in the middle of the procedure I wake up grumbling of pain. As I open my drowsy eyes, I notice on the screen how the tweezers pull a piece of my intestine's wall and bleeding starts. "I can feel it." I let the doctor know. "I need more anesthesia." After the nurse is indicated by the doctor to give another dosage, I close my eyes again and trust that everything is ok just like the past ten years. The usual, is my thought. As the day of December 19th gets dark, I start to worry about the frequent visits to the restroom and some sort of mild abdominal pain. But I do not mention anything to anybody.

At dawn, my body felt like a thousand tons of rock had been deposited on me, I am extremely weak, almost unable to get up off the bed I built on the floor with a thick bed comforter. My kids' dad has already left for his Mexico trip. My one-and-a-half-year-old laying on the floor with me. It is amazing how instinctively he seems to know *mami* is not doing well, Favian does not leave my side at all, he is kissing me all over my face as he holds my hand with all his strength. He seems to predict what is already happening here, I am in denial. I want to have a happy Christmas time with my two children. I am also notoriously preoccupied about my health. The pain increased through the night and the bleeding has not stopped. I do not know what is going on. I cannot even carry my baby nor take care of my four-and-a-half-year-old. Dragging myself on the carpet I reach out for the after-procedure sheet instructions given to me after I left my gastroenterologist office yesterday.

On it I read the following:

Don't drive or make important decisions or go back to work for the rest of the day. If your doctor removed a polyp during your colonoscopy, you may be advised to eat a special diet temporarily. You may feel bloated or pass gas for a few hours after the exam, as you clear the air from your colon.

When should you call for help?

- Call 911 anytime you think you may need emergency care. For example, call if:
- You passed out (lost consciousness) or feel like you will faint.
- You pass a lot of blood from your rectum.
- You have trouble breathing.

Call your doctor or nurse call line now or seek immediate medical care if:

- You have pain that does not get better, even after passing gas.
- You are sick to your stomach or cannot drink fluids.
- You have new or worse belly pain.
- You have blood in your stools.
- You have a fever (over 38°C or 100.4°F).
- You cannot pass stools or gas.

Watch closely for changes in your health, and be sure to contact your doctor or nurse at ...

My thoughts went in so many different directions. At seven am, right when the doctor's office is supposedly open, I dial and a nurse on call picks up, "Hello my name is Susana M. I just had a colonoscopy done yesterday in the morning and currently I am still bleeding. I am feeling extremely weak. My baby is right here with me and I can't get up." The nurse offers to have an ambulance pick me up from my home. I rejected it, I am only five minutes away from the main hospital, my dad can take me. I dress as I can and head to the hospital in my dad's old Chevy medium size truck in the middle of a heavy snowstorm. I give a "see you later" kiss to my children who are staying with my pregnant sister-in-law. At this point I am already feeling better. As soon as I get to the hospital nurses administer some kind of drug to minimize the pain and fluids to get me stronger since I lost a lot of blood by now. A couple hours went by, I just want to go home, I am way better now after all. But the doctors have not found anything yet.

My dad is right there by my side. Growing up, my brothers and I barely saw my father. He spent over 90% of the year in the United States. But he is with me now and that makes me feel loved and strong, this shall pass, yes will pass. It's been over fourteen hours and nobody from the emergency department knows what is going on with me. I am desperate to see my *hijos*, to hug them and continue our lives as usual, together. Right at around 10:30 pm my dad and I are the only people left in the ER. Oh gosh, how embarrassing. I am the only patient left in that dark long hall waiting to be released. Far in the distance, I can hear steps of someone approaching. Who might that be? Another nurse? Perhaps a doctor ready to let me go home? While that silhouette gets closer and closer, I can appreciate a tall man wearing a white gown with a rather disconsolate face expression. His shoulders are hunched like a child feeling guilt after doing something wrong. My spirit was still positive, "I am going home."

With a smile on my face, I let the doctor get closer to where my dad and I are hungerly awaiting. He grabbed a chair and placed it by my side. His first words were, "I am sorry." as he bent his head in sorrow. *No entiendo*, I just want to go home to be with my *hijos*. "In order to save your life, we need to operate on you immediately," he explains but I could not translate that to my dad. How in the world I, his only daughter, going to tell him he is about to lose his only daughter? *Me rehusó, aceptarlo.* I refuse to accept this situation, I refuse to die right now, no, not today, not when Christmas is around the corner. No, "what about my *hijos*?", I screamed. Am I going to be home by Christmas?

NOOOOOOOOOOO! My scream is heard miles away from the emergency room. A devastating scream of a Latina Woman who has a whole world of joy ahead of her. A scream of terror to imagine for a second that I am not going to see, hug, kiss, and tell my *hijos* how much I love them ever again. A scream that penetrates deep into my and my dad's bones.

And there I was, *frente a frente con mi sutil amiga, la muerte.* A friend I am seeing for the first time in my life. A friend who is here to take me into a better place. *Me rehuso,* I am a descendent of the most powerful warriors, the Aztecs. My heart is brave and courageous. My soul is a walking body of hope, faith. My spirit, a woman of color, Latina who won't be defeated by no circumstance she has does not allow. Nothing, nobody is stopping me from redirecting my fate, my *hijos'* fate. I surrender to this experience and accept all the challenges to raise as a phoenix bird, with wider wings to fly far away from hell, to reunite with the glory that has forever been waiting for me. Just like my ancestors the Aztecs did, I honor you my dear friend, death, you are my only hope to liberate the greatness lying within me.

A profound silence invaded the whole intensive care room. My dad has been by my side this whole time, and my mom is taking care of my babies. I lost sense of time, it has probably been days since my surgery, I am alive, I am alive, say it again my dear *valiente guerrera*, I am alive! There are a lot of people going in and out of my room, friends, family, etc., visiting and checking on how I am doing. Wow, I thought I was alone. Even when the murmurs of preoccupation about my life being done, or the many conversations going on right by me, I am experiencing an empowering stillness. I have never experienced this before. Could it be this a way of God to show me that I have a lot of love? That I am love? That remains as a mystery. One thing is for sure, since today, I am making a commitment with the most important person in my life, myself. I am committing to get out of this toxic relationship and continue this journey on my own, with my two angels next to me, Favian and Richy, *LOS AMO.*

Making my way to pursue a higher education as a Latina woman of color and single mom

How do I find my right size pair of shoes? *Chicas*, if I had to go through all of this suffering again, I wouldn't mind. Does it mean that you need to go through the same bumpy muddy road I did to become self-aware? No, not at all. We all have different ways to evolve and mine was this way. Being raised mainly by my mom, who was my first role model as a strong woman, I learned a lot about braking fear chains, stereotype chains, gender chains, cultural chains and more. Beginning in my little rancho I had the privilege to be surrendered with *chicas guerreras*, my neighbors who continue on smiling even within an abusive relationship pretending that *todo* is fine to avoid being criticized by our community. My grandma who taught me that resigning to a life of pain is not the healthiest option a woman should take. My aunts, who became the exception of all by standing up for their beliefs and mainly for their value. My *tio* is eighty-three years old and still very energetic. Boy I want to be like when I grow up. From him, I learned that there is always a bright side to every situation; that with perseverance, I could and can reach the higher level I desire. To my whole little town, that with their unconscious racism from the colonists, taught me to be tough and proud. To the few coaches and mentors and counselors who saw and still see that genius in me, who like me, believe I am a leader to my worth as a woman of color within a colorful culture. Oh gosh, and those long never ending *surcos* of the fields, where I developed a perspective of life greater than what any of us could ever have imagined.

Turning my eyes towards my role models from back in my Guanajuato town and then in the United States, is when I started to recognize the leader in me. Many of them are not even my same skin color or culture or ethnic background or even social-economic status. Some of them have way more tools than I do. One thing is for sure though, I learned to use that in my favor and convert those cultural differences and struggles into the highest ladder I could ever climb. I am a victor not a victim of any circumstances. I take complete responsibility for myself. I recognize my value as a Latina, as a single mom, as a woman of color to continue evolving up the ladder of transformation. Do I still have something left inside me of that little *morenita mexicana* girl? Absolutely, I am her protector, her main solid anchor. I am her guide to a transformation of a more skilled wiser version of herself. It is my genes after all, my ancestors would not permit any limiting beliefs, religion, or language barrier to prevent me from continuing with my life purpose, as a humble proud WOMAN.

Over the years I have found that there is a very fine line between being a victor and a victim. Life is full of choices. The two choices I identify are, you either remain in that jail of your fears to be judged or free yourself into the unknown, into what you actually are and want to be. Once I crossed that line, believe me there is no way back. After reaching a fulfilling state of mind, how could I commit suicide consciously aware of the consequences not only for me, but for my babies too? It is just not consolable in my heart. My life has equipped me with the most unbreakable tools by converting me into a resilient Latina. All those life lessons through the many hardship experiences I have gone through, did not happen in vain.

Did this transformation happen overnight? *Para nada!* Was it ache less? *Menos!* How did I wake up the brilliance in me? Let's go just a little bit back to when I was diagnosed with stage four cancer. Along this physical treatment a huge internal shift occurred within my being. When going through chemo, I received a lot of input from outsiders, including one that assured, from innocence and skepticism that this was a punishment from God. A punishment??? The divine is our father, and just like we are mothers, we want the best for our children, but have little control over their decisions. Just like a mother or father, the divine has been always there to guide and hold my hand during tough times. You know, I thank this person. They made me realize that cancer was actually a blessing and opportunity for me to evolve and become a better spiritual being living a human life.

A los 28 años, so young I have gone through so much. Later, I understood this happens when your apparent reality does not match your authentic inner self. Then that false picture of what a woman must be, turns into an autoimmune disease, which was eating me alive.

Along the way, I discovered the power of literature. I autodidactically educated myself on so many different topics. At the beginning, it was mainly about, "Why does a human hurt other humans?" I was trying to understand my partner at the time, where did all this hateful behavior toward me and my children come from. As time passed, a specialist on families suggested that I also get to know myself, which is where the magic of transformation began. I started to read books, watch videos, and became the most meticulous observant of my surroundings. At first nothing made sense. I just did what the authors who have had experiences similar to mine suggested to get them out of their suffering cycle. I came to realize that the most important person in my life was not my then husband, nor my children, but ME. I acknowledge it was quite a shock for me. I had been raised as the compliant and meek woman that I'm supposed to be. Thinking about myself as the most important person in my life when all I knew was everybody comes first, was a tremendous shift. As I deepened more into literature and the history of women's oppression, the more I convinced myself of healing in order to help my adorable children to do the same. I started to see me as a true role model for them. So, my real job is to evolve and develop the appropriate skills from them to follow. So, I did.

This evolutionary process took nights and days, months and years of undusting buried authenticity. It took lots of self-reflection, more reading, self-monitoring, lots of observation of myself and others, investigating different scenarios, it was an incessant learning journey of change, which continues to be up until this day. The more I got to know and define my true self, the more curious I became. Reading topics on self-love, how to deal with a divorce, how to talk to my *hijos* about their parents' separation, how to help them heal at such a young age, how to prepare them for what they will encounter in the hands of our cruel society. I wrote what I pictured my lovely family to be and it became our reality. I created a daily routine which took me from illness to wellness by teaching my soul and over all my body my cells and neurons how to heal and reprogram. Many of my close friends started to call me resilient, so I became a maven on the topic, which has become my nature. I started to teach my children and everyone around me about what I have learned throughout these life adventures and how by changing my perspective towards life changed my life taking me and my two sons to a state of peace of mind.

A grieving process has been part of this evolution, you gotta own it in order to grow. Let me tell you though, the more you practice the easier it is to go through it faster enough to react right on time. You must own it!!! The only way to get out of my own trap was accepting that I am the only one, at least 99% of it, responsible for my own suffering or happiness. This is easy to say, it is a totally different thing to actually do it. Unfortunately, humans' ego gets in between our own personal development, in between that reconnection with the SELF. I hated me at some point in my life, now I know it was part of the grieving process of leaving behind who I thought I was to become the real me with some updated modifications of my own. I discovered that we are energy, now that was a true shock, and that our crazy thoughts, 7, 000 per day to be exact, develop some kind of emotion, this one could be a negative dramatic emotion or a joyful, hopeful emotion, which I also discover I have the control over how I want to feel about certain thought either real or made up. I made the discovery that by staying aligned with my mind, soul, spirit and physical body, I could take my potential to a totally higher level of self-consciousness.

Now, this conscious and subconscious topic is very delicate in our Latino and many other cultures, societal norms, politics, religions, culture and more caused me an unimaginable blooding journey when it came to reconnect with my inner self. I know what I describe is an illusionary torture. I literally assassinate the false version of me, by "disconnecting from everything to connect to everything." *Susie Mosqueda, 2006.* I created a different version of me. As a Latina Woman of color, I can assure you that I am limitless. I am by instinct taking all the opportunities that this amazing country and the world offers us which better serve my divine purpose. Showing the way less troubled by Latinas like myself. The popular phrase "enjoy the process" has a meaningful weight for those *guerreras* who let their wild *chica* out. Am I done here? No, my story continues.

My eyes are open wider today till forever

I see new colors to create innovative combinations.

… and I finally got it. I am able to reach my goals. I must be wearing the right shoes, the invincible *guerrera* shoes!

My message to women and humans out there, *hermosas guerreras valientes,* what about you, when are you starting your liberation?

When are you starting to get ready to receive the many blessings holding on for you on the other side of pain, FEAR?

I invite you to take action NOW, find the right pair of shoes for you, because NOW is the time!

I'm evermore thankful and I invite you to connect with me any given day.

I'm always here to GIVE back and have your back!

Susie Mosqueda is a self-made immigrant LATINA who has overcome many challenges on her way to success. She is known by many as an unstoppable warrior and a phoenix that has emerged from the ashes, triumphant, with a solid resilient inner strength. Susie is the founder of the IDENTI-DAD program, which supports women to reconnect with their inner BRILLIANCE through the alignment of their body, mind, and soul. She has impacted hundreds of women globally. Susie's transformational techniques bring quick life-changing results and those she mentors feel and see a substantial positive effect in a short period of time. Additionally, her clients and mentees learn the tools of mastering self-motivation, sense of self, and develop an intrinsic interest in implementing the autodidact learning modality into their daily lives.

CHAPTER 8
TOLU

Rethinking Failure
Learning To Receive Unconditional Love

Growing up in a profoundly dysfunctional and abusive environment, I developed many coping mechanisms that I didn't know deeply impacted me as a person.

My father has rewired the definition of failure in my heart and head. Recently, I had to do a certification exam. I was so nervous about it because it was the first test I had done in quite a long time. The timeline for the exam was short. It was during the holiday season. I had recently gone through some stressful and significant changes in my personal and professional life. These were massive changes amid COVID, yet I attempted a significant feat studying for this exam with an aggressive timeline. I told my husband that I was afraid to fail.

He said to me, 'It's okay.'

Me: It's not okay. I cannot fail.

Him: It's okay if you fail.

Me: No, it is not. At this point, my frustration was almost choking me in tears.

Here I was, an accomplished woman with two advanced degrees where I passed rigorous professional exams and yet, so scared of a certification.

Him: If you fail, you learn from it and try again.

Me: I won't try again if I fail. I am done!

Him: Why? A failure doesn't define you. If you fail, that is why I am here, to absorb your losses and magnify your success.

Me: I looked up at him with hope in my eye for the first time.

Taking in his words. All the while, I had been looking down and away, which is a posture of shame. I was yet to do the exam. I had not even failed, yet I was already exhibiting shame at the thought of it.

I thought to myself, absorb my failures, and magnify my success? No one has ever said those words to me before.

"You should be proud of yourself for even trying," he continued. "Many people are not trying to do what you are doing. You should be proud. It's the holidays when many are partying and relaxing, and I see you here studying daily. It is enviable. Whatever the outcome is, know that you are loved. I love you, and that will never change based on the result of a test. The test result doesn't define you".

It suddenly felt like fresh air was pushed through my lungs. I could breathe easy again. I felt my heart rate lower as I sank into the loving embrace of my husband, taking in all the love he has for me. I knew at that moment that I had enough courage to face the exam and would be fine irrespective of the outcome. It was a strange feeling. A different kind of attitude towards failure. If you knew my history, you would see that this was a significant shift for me; A PHENOMENAL LIFE-CHANGING SHIFT in my heart.

Failure was a taboo word in my upbringing. As the first of five children, I was the yardstick for perfection. I could never fail. I could never do anything wrong because, God forbid, my siblings see that I failed and then go on to fail. Failure was not welcome, nor spoke of and often severely punished. So, as a young child, I was aggressively motivated, albeit by the wrong thing- I MUST NOT FAIL. Failure attracted dire consequences. It was a toxic comparison. It was either I was first, best, or don't come home. I am not sure how it started with me as a young child, but my earliest memory was something like this.

I grew up in a British educational system where class positions were given based on grade. If there were 20 people in the class, students get a position from 1st, 2nd, 3rd, 15th to 20th. I had to be first with a high percentage at all times.

If I was second, my father asked me why I wasn't 1st, even if my 2nd position had a cumulative percentage of 99.9%. If I was 1st with a sub-optimal percentage like 95%, my father asked me why it wasn't higher even though I was first in the entire class. I was always to do better, to be better, and nothing was ever enough or applauded or celebrated.

This led me to become an adult who never appreciated how hard she worked, how smart she was, or how to celebrate her successes. Celebration felt flimsy, and I am still working on that. It was almost taboo to enjoy anything in my upbringing, even my hard-earned success. The narrative was almost as if – IF I CELEBRATE, I WILL LAPSE AND FAIL.

So, I have lived a life full of achievements but barely ever stopped to enjoy any of them. Because of this background, failure was never talked about in my home. I grew up with tremendous pressure to perform.

My worst experience with failure happened in my final year of high school. It wasn't a failure actually; it was the failure to meet a metric goal initially, which further cemented my attitude to success.

In my home country, the educational system involved taking national entry exams to determine what university and program of study you got. Right from when I was a child, I had always been told by my dad that I should be a Medical Doctor. He said to me several times that I was smart, and that is what I will become.

This formed a lot of decisions in my life. These were not decisions I made myself because I didn't have freedom of choice in that home. My dad made my decisions.

Getting into University in my country involved filling out a form and submitting it by mail. As a potential student, you had three choices of university and three choices of a program to fill in. The idea behind this is to allow you alternatives to be considered if you do not need the cut-off mark for a specified university or degree program. For example, if the cut-off mark to be admitted for Medicine in a 'University 1' is 270 out of 300, and your score is 245, you will be not be considered for Medicine. You may be considered for your degree options 2 and 3 for the same University if the cut-off mark fits. For example, Bachelors's in microbiology or physiology. If the cut off mark for Medicine is in University 2 and 3 is 250 and 240 respectively, it means that you may get to be admitted for Medicine in University 3 but a Bachelors in Microbiology in 'University 1', you pick! If your score was 230, for example, and doesn't meet any of the requirements to be admitted into University 1, 2, or 3, you fall out! It was a ranking system and highly competitive because it was national and also regional. There weren't a lot of schools with a degree in Medicine.

A degree in Medicine is very competitive to get. They were only a few colleges in the entire country with Medical Schools. In addition, the more reputable a school, the more competitive it gets. As a result, such a reputable school with Medicine as a degree further raises its barrier to entry by raising its cut-off mark. My dad wanted me to go to the best school, to study Medicine in the most reputable, most sought-after university in the entire country. The odds were indeed against me.

Here was the issue. I was 15 years old when I had my first test to get into Medical School. It was a major exam. I didn't have extra coaching or my textbooks. I didn't even know how to prepare for the exam. There was a lot of pressure on me. The national exam was stage 3 of getting into medical school. There were two exams in high school that also determined my future; exam 1 and 2 results would prove to the world that I had strong enough grades to get into any science major, especially Medicine.

I had to study for and pass both of these exams within a few months of each other. I had a month gap between them while taking care of four younger siblings. Unfortunately, I also was a mother to my mom. I didn't know how much pressure I was under until I had my first asthma attack as a teenager between major (determine-my-future) exams 1 and 2. I remember clearly clutching my chest as I crawled towards the door of the house, gasping for air, trying to mouth words to call a neighbor, fearing I was about to die. I had never had an asthma attack before then. I remember being under so much pressure of excelling/not failing any exam, including the subjects in liberal arts and language. Even though the subjects were not going to be used to determine if I got into medical school or not, I was not allowed to have less than a distinction in any subject in my home; so, I labored.

Between helping my siblings with their homework, cooking for the family, cleaning, handwashing the entire family's laundry, running errands (all of this without the use of any form of technology for ease and speed), I had to study and ace every homework assignment in addition to these major exams which determine whether or not I got into medical school. With all the chores and household responsibilities, studying was hard. After spending hours in the hot sun hand washing the laundry to the entire family, I asked my dad why he won't ask my younger brother, who was 13 at the time, to help out by doing some of his laundry. My dad flared and cursed at me. When I told him that

I needed help so that I could have some time to study and ace the upcoming tests, he got even madder at the idea that I would suggest to him to lighten my household chores.

I had no help or encouragement, or a role model. I was the first-born, so no one had gotten into college before me. There was no Medical Doctor in my family history, so I had no one to look up to. I was going to be first. I had no guidance. I had no idea what doctors did or what their training involved. At that time of my life, my memory of Medical Doctors was people who wore a white coat, sat on a chair in their office, and said, "Next!". I think whatever questions were asked, my mom answered. I hadn't been to the doctor a lot in my life because most of my common ailments were fixed with over-the-counter medications, so I didn't have any frequent or long-term interaction with any medical doctor. All I knew was that my dad wanted me to be a Medical Doctor, and I must not fail.

When the time came to apply to colleges around the country, my dad filled my forms. Most students filled it themselves or with their parents' help, but he filled the form himself. The results from national exams 1 and 2 determined if I could even consider exam 3 and put Medicine as a field of study. I had distinctions in Biology, Chemistry, Biology, Maths, and other subjects I didn't even need to get into medical school for exams 1 and 2, but I wasn't in the clear yet.

Exam 3 was my final sentence, as I called it back then. Results of exam 3 determined if I would be offered admission to medical school, between, note that admission into medical school didn't decide whether you will study Medicine. There were a few years of dancing on hot stones of fire until you got into the clinical year; until then, failure at any state could throw you out of medical school.

The exam was a standardized exam and heavily proctored. I undertook this exam at 15 years of age, not knowing how to prepare for such a high-stakes national standardized exam, and did not make the cut-off for Medicine in University 1. I made about 87% of what would be considered a minimum cut-off for this school. There was no consideration for Medicine. The school offered me Cell Biology and Genetics (CBG) as an alternative, my dad turned it down. He didn't ask if I would consider it or what I thought.

Before I continue my narration, I must let you know that I have forgiven my dad of all these past ills and do have a respectable relationship with my biological dad; it is not intimate, but it is present. Something to note is that it is indeed a miracle that I would have an existing relationship with my dad, and even a respectable one considering the deep trauma he has caused in my life.

Back to the story, I recall my dad saying to me, "Medicine or nothing!" He declined on my behalf. University 2 offered me a microbiology degree, with a potential consideration in 2nd year to transfer to Medicine if my scores were insanely high enough. My dad declined once again. Another route to get into medical school at University 1, which was the Advanced Diploma route. It involved another exam; this exam was University-specific. This prestigious University came up with this pathway of entry, which was more expensive as an alternative to the national exam.

While this was a public university with a considerable fee for the middle-class population to afford tuition for their children, the Advanced Diploma route was a ruthless eliminator. About

20 students from the entire student applicant would be considered for Medicine. The 20 included other majors like Dentistry, Physiotherapy, etc. The potential 20 students were not all medical students. The final barrier was cost. Tuition for the first year was ten times higher than regular tuition.

I had the second-highest score out of thousands of students who applied for the Advanced Diploma route. Unfortunately, I couldn't get into that school because of cost. My dad couldn't afford it.

Consequentially, I had to wait another year to apply to Medical School. It was painful for a lot of reasons that I wouldn't go into.

Gap Year

For a year, I stayed at home wondering how to not fail the next exam. During this forced gap year, I graduated high school. My house chores remained the same or increased because I was home. I still had no study tools. I thought perhaps having a textbook would help me do better in Chemistry test scores. I had gone through school, generally without having all my textbooks. To boost my scores in chemistry, I got a used chemistry text book. I self-studied mostly using question banks.

At some point, my dad enrolled me in Computer Programming degree program to keep me from being at home all the time. I aced the class. I sort of enjoyed it, but I wasn't allowed to pursue it further. I got a part-time teaching job to teach high schoolers science subjects. From this job, I saved a bit of money to cater for my wardrobe. My first purchase as a teenage girl was a brown wedge sandal. I was so proud of myself for being able to buy something with my hard-earned income.

The day my dad saw me wearing these three-inch wedge sandals, he began to berate me. He said things like, "You have no common sense; instead of you to be ashamed of failing to get into medical school, you are focusing on fashion. This shoe makes you look awkward. Your legs are not straight. It doesn't suit you. If there is a shootout, you will not be able to run. This is nonsense." He ordered me to take off my shoes and hand them over to him.

It was my first time wearing the shoe. He took them from me, poured gas on it, and set them on fire. He burned my shoes!

It was the first time I ever wore them. It was my first non-flat shoe and my last for a very long time. I still struggle a bit with heels. I still remember those deathly words he spoke to me.

Unfortunately, the worst was yet to come. As the dates for the next national exam drew closer, the pressure mounted in my home. For the second time, I applied to study Medicine in this highly prestigious University but this time around, it came with a multi-level threat.

The Second Time Around
There are less than 18 months between my younger brother and me. As a result, I was only ahead of him by 1 yr in school. With my inability to secure a seat to study Medicine and having to wait another year, we were now on the same level. My dad made me feel so much shame about this. My brother was applying for Engineering, I was applying for Medicine and Surgery. It was his first time; it was my second time. Once again, my dad filled out all the forms himself and put in Medicine as degree options 1, 2, and 3 and the University's name as school options 1, 2, and 3. This strategy was dangerous in the sense that, should I fail to

make the cut-off mark for Medicine for that school, I would have no other options. My fate was sealed.

My dad came to me one evening and said, "Make sure that you get into Medicine in this school and that you score higher than your brother in this national exam. If you don't fulfill these two conditions, leave my house and don't return". Not only did I have to get into a super competitive program for Medicine, I also had to one-up my brother, who isn't even seeking to be in the same program as I was and who didn't need as high of a score. "My life is over," I thought. "This was almost impossible."

Why do I say this?

There are a lot of factors that determine if I get into medical school aside from having a high score. Because it's a national exam at various centers all over the country on the same day, if a center is suspected of cheating, the entire center's score is grounded. It is not released, regardless of whether you had anything to do with the exam malpractice or not. They were a lot of variables at play that was beyond my control.

What if I was unlucky and found myself in such a center? If I aced my exam, we would never know. How can I control or ensure that I was able to get into this University to study Medicine? Why use my brother as an ultimatum? We didn't have the same major subjects for this national exam. The questions were also shuffled. Having those requirements to be seen as a daughter worthy enough to live in my dad's house was confoundingly sad.

The exam day came. There was tension everywhere. Some things weren't optimal at the exam center. One of these was that my dad had suggested getting "help" to me during the exam to ensure I passed. I declined. It was a challenging exam. I was uncertain and destabilized. In the beginning, they got my major wrong and gave me the wrong set of questions, which was later retracted 45 mins into the exam. At that point, I was given fresh sets of questions with no extra time for the time defects. I was very panicked. The 'arranged help' came to try to provide me with answers to exam questions. I declined again.

After the exam, my brother and I went out to meet our dad. We got into the car to go home. My dad placed my brother in the front and me in the back. He spoke to my brother alone and ignored me. It was a long exam. My brother and I were both famished, but my dad never asked me what I would like to eat. He asked my brother and got him a snack. I was confused about why I was being ignored, though it was a familiar punishment strategy. Emotional neglect and malice were some of the ways he punished me, so I knew something was wrong.

For me, the drive home was silent as my heartbeat wildly in my chest, anxiously pondering what awaited me when we got home.

It was one of my other brother's birthdays that Saturday. When we got home, the smell of fried rice greeted us. My mom was cooking in the kitchen. The fried rice was a special meal of celebration; it wasn't a meal we ate regularly. There was no power in the house that night. I used to live in a country with regular power outages.

The exam was an entire day affair. We probably left the house at four am before the center was far from the city; we were now getting home at about eight pm, tired and still famished. As soon as we got home, my dad said to me, "Give me your hand."

He had a cane in his hand, ready to flog me. Panicking, I wondered what I did. I mean, we just got home. Of course, I submitted and gave him my hand, but his fury was overwhelming.

He beat me all over my body. I was cornered.

He said things like, 'You want to destroy your life. I sent you to help you refused. You are very stubborn. If you don't pass and get into medical school, get out of my house. I don't want a nuisance'. In case you are wondering, So, my dad was beating me because I refused to cheat in my exam.

I recall that I wasn't just crying. I was groaning, in pain and agony, with tears gushing out of my face. As a 16-year-old, even I was shocked by the kind of sounds coming out of my throat. I remember sobbing, going into my mother's room in the dark, kneeling down by the bed and praying to God.

"God, I am like the Israelites in the bible," I prayed. "I am asking for help. Please save me from my oppressor. Help me pass so I can get into medical school. I don't want to be on the streets. Help me get into medical school. Help me score higher than my brother", I prayed.

All the while, I was groaning in tears. I cannot call it crying because the audible sound from my mouth was that of deep distress. I prayed to God to help me meet the metrics of my dad so that I would not end in the streets.

Nobody came into the room. Not even my mom. She didn't even try to save me when my dad was beating me for fear of being accused of contributing to the destruction of my life.

When the results were released, I did pass the exam. I got into this prestigious University on merit to study Medicine. I also had a higher score than my brother. Both prayers got answered. However, the fear of failure went on to torment me for the rest of my teenage years and into adulthood.

In graduate school, I won awards for leadership, excellence, major scholarships, and also convocation speaker. It was the first time I recall hearing the word, 'I am proud of you" from my dad. Yet, at the same time, he continually expressed disappointment for being single longer than my dad would like. Being single as a woman in my birth country was heavily frowned upon, especially when you are of "marriageable age." I was often made to feel like I committed a crime. In the end, I left my home country when I was almost forcefully married to a man I barely knew

So, here I was, an accomplished woman who still didn't carry much value in my dad's eyes because I was single. The love and affection felt very transactional. My dad was proud of me when I met a specific metric in his eyes, and then suddenly, I was a nonentity when I didn't. This interaction gave me a false metric of value for me as a person. There were many seasons of my life where I desired something but the fear of failure kept me from trying. I couldn't bear the thought of failing, even if the only person who knew that I failed was me. The thought tormented me and kept me from pursuing my desires.

Later in life, while living in the United States, I went for a 2nd advanced degree. My first semester coming out of a British educational system, I took 4 classes, which was considered a suicide mission even by the American students who were familiar with the system. I tend to be very ambitious, and felt it was nothing.

I had failed to consider that I was in a new culture, climate, educational system, and, as a result, should make allowance for adjustments. The semester ended with me having a "B' grade in one of my subjects, which was quite unsettling to me. I felt like a failure and was complaining to an American student. The next semester, I had all "A" s but had an "A-"in one of the subjects. The "A-"felt like a punch in the gut. I hated the minus sign because to me if something was missing from me. I complained to the same American student who happened to be in one of my study groups. After the 3rd semester and I complained about another "A-"minus, she said to me, "Why do you get so upset at an A-minus. You came here from another country to a different educational system, taking more classes than most American students. You have had to adjust to the climate, culture, people, way of living. You don't have a family support system, and you are having A's. I am an American student who does not have all these challenges and only get Bs, you should be proud of yourself and all your accomplishments".

When she said this to me, it shifted my perspective about what I labeled "failure." I was so hard-wired to see anything less than perfection is a failure, so much so that I mocked my own efforts. While my classmate helped keeps things in perspective, it still didn't rid me of the fear of failure or feeling like a failure completely when things aren't perfect. As I continued into my adult life, I constantly never saw my achievements as anything if they were not perfect. A mindset that would not be replaced until later through my loving relationship with my husband as an adult.

When I met my future husband, I was sick and didn't know if and how long it would take me to recover. I wasn't sure if I'll ever be a productive member of society again, and I told him so. That didn't deter him. I didn't want to be in a relationship as I feared that he would judge me by where I was. I would have been open to a relationship if he knew me when I was in my "best season," but in this state, "No," was my thought. I didn't want any man to look down on me for anything.

When I was dating my husband, whenever we would meet, he always welcomed me with open hands and a big broad smile on his face like a father happy to see his daughter coming home. For some reason, his arms felt more gigantic than they were, and receiving hugs was strange to me, for I was never hugged as a child or as a teenager or adult by my parents. Here, I was courting a man who loved to give and receive hugs.

It was uncomfortable.

One day, I was doing all I could to break up with him and said something like, "I may never be able to work in my life, and you would have to support me. I may never be able to do this…I may never be able to that…." I spurted out in anger.

With tears in his eyes, he took my face in his hands gently and said, "And…so…what? So what? Your worth isn't determined by what you do or do not do. Your worth isn't determined by your achievements. I am glad I met you here, at this time and now. I am proud of you and all that you have achieved already. It is incredible,".

I stared back in disbelief, thinking to myself, "This is the strangest man I have ever met'.

When we got married, it was hard. I couldn't bear not being

productive and contributing to my family, but my physical health at the time wasn't optimal. One of the issues I struggled with was sleep. He would say to me, "Don't worry about anything, my love, just lay down and try to sleep." This man-made sleep his daily goal for me? This was a far cry from my upbringing and experience with my dad, where I would be chastised for sleeping in or not working. To not be seen doing something in my dad's house growing up attracted animosity of some sort. The worth was on how much you produced. Here my husband just wanted me to be well. For months, his first question to me every day was, "did you sleep," even now, with years in, his first question to me every day is, "did you sleep well?"

His love for me has changed my life.
I am easier to talk to.
I am more receptive to other's ideas and opinions while holding my own steadily.
With him, I didn't need to prove anything.
With him, my soul could rest.
With him, my lungs felt lighter.
With him, my smile got richer.
With time, I got better!

Today, I am a whole, healed, and functional, productive member of society, which I attribute a lot of my healing to my husband's love for me. As I write this, I glanced at my Fitbit, and I have had weeks of good sleep with no sleep medicine. I have had higher sleep scores for weeks in a row, which is a miracle. I AM THRIVING.

When faced with this recent exam, I wanted to do for certification, and the old fears came back again. Just a word from my husband calmed all my fears. I knew that I would be able to carry on with my daily activities irrespective of the test's outcome because I KNOW that I am deeply, deeply loved.

It is in how he serves me.
It's in how he looks at me.
It is in how he talks about me.
He affirms all my good.
He is My calmer half.
He is My assurance in the face of the storm.
He is My best friend.

Because of my husband's unconditional love and belief in me, I am finally entering a season of my life where I am working on being a FULL-BLOWN WRITER and ENTREPRENEUR, something I knew existed in me, but I was too afraid to try. I was scared of being seen, heard, or known. I was afraid to fail. I was also scared to succeed at anything different than being a Medical Doctor.

It is a brand-new start for me. It is time for rest and restoration.

Tolu Oyewumi (M.D., M.P.H.) is different by design. By resilience, while confronting and overcoming some significant life challenges, she attained two advanced degrees before the age of 30 to be a Physician and Epidemiologist. Yet, she still felt like a failure and was unfulfilled. Accomplishing hard things personally and professionally never made her feel like she was enough. Consistently troubled by a sense of what "failure" and "success" looked like as predetermined and conditioned by her childhood, she decided to take her healing journey into her hands. The goal was to KNOW, UNDERSTAND, LOVE, and AFFIRM herself.

A significant realization on this journey was her inability to receive love and how empty her love jar was. All her life, she had loved, served, and gave to others consistently; as the first of five, then being in a caregiving career as a Physician, and being that "responsible person" everyone runs to for help. She was very good at giving but not receiving, a sore spot in her life that consistently came up for air after meeting her now-husband. Her story is an example of how she is navigating self-love against all odds.

Dr. Oyewumi is also a Certified Coach, Public Speaker, Creative Writer, Youth Mentor. She is happily married to her best friend and lover, Josh. She tries to live a balanced life by incorporating things she enjoys, such as reading non-fiction, watching action-themed movies, spending time alone. She longs to be a voice in an animated film in the future.

CHAPTER 9

HEATHER

We thought starting a family would be easy.

This is the story of a husband and wife starting a family. It's not an unfamiliar story given the millions of couples who have had the same desire. However, the process can look very different in different couples. For my husband Elmer and I, we saw our pursuit as the most natural thing we would ever do. Knowing this, we started trying—and make no mistake, *trying* is the fun part. We chose not to add pressure by tracking ovulation cycles or using other scientific methods. We just did what came naturally. Months into our pursuit—success! We were pregnant.

At that time, we were stationed in Cambridge, England, away from blood relatives and friends in the United States. Despite this, we had the love and support of local military friends and "church family". Interestingly, it seemed we were about to have a child with dual citizenship. That aside, there was tremendous joy in knowing we had conceived a child. It seemed that the natural process *really* worked!

In the first months of the pregnancy, everything was progressing well. We had an ultrasound at eleven weeks and the baby was growing normally. I was working as a physical therapist in a British hospital and after work. I would come home and take my daily pregnancy naps. I was eating well, sleeping well, and staying healthy. Everything was progressing according to plan. However, we soon discovered that *our* plan did not dictate the pregnancy. What follows here are the actual journal entries from my experience when problems in the pregnancy started to occur.

Journal entry for July 18, 2000.

Today, I seemed to lose quite a bit of mucous, seemingly my mucous plug from the cervix. I wasn't really sure how to react to this occurrence, but the last time I spoke to the midwife about a concern, she suggested I wait for the ultrasound to confirm that all is fine with the baby. I have an ultrasound in the morning, so I may wait until then to see if things are alright.

Journal entry for July 19, 2000.

This morning, I went for the 20-week ultrasound and all was well with the baby. The ultrasonographer found what she called "his bits" indicating that the baby was a little boy. I was a bit surprised, but not disappointed. When I went back to work this afternoon, I went with a word about the mucous plug from the midwife. She said that it could begin to come off at any time and that I needn't worry unless I started to see bright red blood. While at work, I began to get bloody mucous coming down which turned into a regular flow of blood by the evening. As I sat waiting for my husband to get home to take me to the hospital, I tried hard not to panic. I sat in the quiet and began to seek the Lord in the words of the Bible and prayer.

I had not experienced bleeding at any other time during the pregnancy. We knew we had just seen the baby and he was fine, so I tried to calm down about the situation. My husband and I went to the hospital only to find our worst fears confirmed, a late miscarriage. Because it was so late in the pregnancy, it would require a delivery of the fetus to remove him from my body. Who knew that this was how these things worked? We were already made aware that the baby was not a viable fetus, and it was a horrible thing to have to go through delivering a stillborn. But it had to be done. They broke my water manually and administered pitocin, to prompt an early labor. The delivery was quick without much physical pain, but the emotional pain was almost unbearable as we stared at his lifeless body. It was here that our first attempt to have a child ended. So now what?

We had prepared and done what we needed to do to see this through to a better result, but this is what can happen when you're starting a family. No one ever talks about the death of miscarriage, only the joys of pregnancies that result in beautiful new babies. Because of our faith, we refused to be discouraged. I've always been a proponent of the old saying, "If you fall off a horse, you get back on and ride again.". For us, it had to be that way to enjoy the rewards of children. So, we waited the required weeks that the doctor prescribed after the miscarriage to start trying again, and, the "trying" was still the fun part. As it turned out, we had lost the baby boy in July, but were pregnant again by September. Who knew I was a "fertile Myrtle"? Apparently, conceiving a child was not our issue. With grim determination, we set our minds to complete the process *successfully* in this pregnancy.

There were two things that were *absolutely* necessary and encouraging to me this second time around.

One was my husband's love and support. As a dedicated husband would be after our first experience, he did everything he could to help ensure that both me and the baby were healthy. I remember that Christmas, he gave me the most beautiful gift of a figurine with a mother holding her baby's hands to support the first steps of walking. Tears welled up in my eyes as I received that gift knowing he was with me every step of the way in this next pregnancy. The greatest gift is knowing that someone is supporting you in the most loving way possible. I knew I couldn't even venture into pregnancy again without that kind of support.

The second thing that encouraged me and kept me from constant fear and doubt was the dreams that I had of how complete the life of this baby would be. At the time, we did not know the sex of our child, but I was able to experience the baby's life in my dreams. I believe that was a gift that God gave to sustain me through this joyful experience. In fact, it was during that time that I determined if the baby were a girl, her middle name would be Joy.

Days turned into weeks and weeks turned into months. Things were going very well with the pregnancy. In fact, completing week 20 felt like victory because that was the week in the first pregnancy where we had the miscarriage. I remember coming home in the car with my husband at the end of that week celebrating that we had gotten to this point without any problems. Week 21 was another matter. I began to leak fluid and was concerned that it was amniotic fluid. Surely this couldn't be happening again. We went to the emergency room, and our worst fears were confirmed again. I was leaking amniotic fluid and lots of it. Essentially, it was as if my water broke, and we were only in week twenty-one. The ultrasound showed that the baby was fine.

The recommendation of the doctor was to put me on bed rest and see how long I could hold the pregnancy. I was not in active labor and every precious day that the baby could stay in the womb was critical. No one knew how many days that would be, but it could mean the difference between life and death for this child. I was transferred to a hospital that was better equipped for an early birth if it were to happen. Then, the wait began. When I say I was on bed rest, I mean *strict* bed rest. I mainly just got up to use the bathroom. During that time, even my backside got sore from sitting so much. I was determined to do whatever it took to bring this precious child into the world safely.

Prayer all around us intensified. We had the love and support of friends and family from England to the United States, and we remained in the place of faith in God. I remember going for an ultrasound while on bed rest and my husband asking if the sex of the baby could be determined. At that stage, I wasn't pressed about the issue, I just wanted a healthy baby. As it turned out, the sex could not be determined because the baby's legs were not floating sufficiently, given the loss of amniotic fluid. It was like the difference between taking a bath and taking a shower. My body was creating new amniotic fluid every day, but the baby was no longer swimming in it—just being washed in it. The ultrason-agrapher also told us the baby was in breech position with the feet down toward the birth canal.

Three and a half weeks after starting bed rest, labor started. It was a weak labor, and the risk of infection was so high, the doctors were tentative about intervening or even examining me. Not to mention, the cervix was not sufficiently dilated or effaced. So, a decision was made to boost my labor with pitocin. I *really* started feeling it then. I was moving all over the bed—in response to the strong contractions—trying to be set for delivery. I was ready! The midwife offered me "gas" and "air", but I was too far in the process to stop for additional interventions. Although the baby was in breech position, I knew that it was small enough to pass through the birth canal safely. In England, they don't force you to deliver in stirrups. In fact, they encourage to do what comes naturally. For me in that moment, the natural thing to do was to turn my body around and grab the headboard and I delivered the baby on all fours.

Immediately after birth, the contractions ceased. Now I was left wondering about the sex of the baby. There were many doctors and nurses around the warming bed where the baby had been transferred, but no one would tell me what the sex of the baby was! There were many assessments that had to be completed, so I tried to be patient. Eventually, they brought me this little, tiny bundle wrapped in what seemed like a hundred blankets—my precious new daughter. It's a girl! My little Kendra Joy.

I cried tears of joy and she at a tender, gestational age of twenty-four and a half weeks had her eyes wide open looking up at me. She could breathe, she could move her little body, and she was ours. Due to her need for further development in the systems of her body, she had to be put on a ventilator and they whisked her off to the NICU. For me, it was a transfer to the operating room to have the afterbirth removed. When a baby is delivered this early, the afterbirth doesn't always separate from the body as it should and it had to be removed manually. Once that was done, the staff wheeled my entire hospital bed into the NICU to see Kendra on the warming bed in all of her glory. By now, she had lines and tubes coming out of everywhere. My husband and I were still confident that all would be well, but the neonatologists offered us little hope after their assessments. They had the typical "wait-and-see" attitude. The doctors *did* say that girls tend to fare better than boys and African-American babies tend to fare better than other races. With our already firm faith, that was enough to keep us encouraged through the first night of her life.

The next day, hormones and reality hit me hard. I was in tears off and on the whole day knowing the challenges of bonding with a baby I couldn't hold. My husband suggested I accept the hospital's offer to stay in what they called their "parent rooms". This would allow me to stay in the hospital all day and night with a bedroom space that was available and accessible to the NICU. This suggestion only made me more emotional, but I agreed to try.

My first time back in the NICU to see my daughter Kendra was difficult. Not only did I know I couldn't hold her, but her little frail body seemed like she was clinging to life and struggling to breathe. Her legs were so tiny, I could've put my wedding ring around her foot and ankle in one motion. In her first baby photo, she was curled up in the fetal position with my husband's open hand behind her. She could fit in his hand with room to spare. The hospital weighed her in at one pound and eight ounces and she measured eleven inches long. I knew I had to settle in my heart how to get through this experience. Fortunately, in England, hospitals are willing to see you through the process for as long as it takes. The neonatologists estimated four months, which would take her up to the original due date. Of course, it was all based on whether she survived. There were many babies in the NICU who were coming and going daily and some of those goings were not discharges home but to heaven. As parents in these difficult circumstances, we all determined to encourage one another. The nursing staff was outstanding with their care and encouragement. Even with that, I knew I had to have a plan to get me through everything it was going to take in order to get my child home. I had faith in my heart from the dreams God had given me, that she would recover.

Part of what helped me stay on task was my decision to breast-feed. I had planned to nurse the baby early on in the pregnancy but now under this difficult circumstance—where Kendra was being fed through a tube—it was even more challenging. Four times a day, I sat with the automatic machine expressing milk. I yielded quite a bit in those first few weeks. The nurses called the first milk after delivery "liquid *gold*". It contained critical immunity factors and nutrients that would benefit babies during health challenges. In the hospital unit, I was able to freeze my growing supply of breast milk because Kendra was only getting syringe amounts at a time. Apparently, I built up quite a supply in their freezer and the nurses asked me if I would be willing to donate some of the milk to other babies. I gladly agreed, knowing that I had relationships with other parents who had children that were in need of this supply. It was better than formula for good recovery. So, after a few simple blood tests, I was a cleared to donate my supply of milk. My husband joked that I was a "wet nurse" for the NICU, but donating the milk definitely helped me focus on something positive.

Several weeks into Kendra's hospital stay, we received a box from the ladies auxiliary assigned to the hospital. It was filled with the most precious little baby doll dresses, knit hats, socks, and sweaters that you could imagine. At the time, even store-bought preemie clothes were too big for Kendra, and it was such a blessing to have this gift as a way to cover her little body once she had some of the lines removed.

About one month into our stay, surgery was up for discussion. The artery in Kendra's body that was meant to close after birth to allow for proper heart and lung blood circulation had not closed. The issue occurred because of her premature birth. She would need to have the artery closed in order to continue to function normally. By this time, she was only about three pounds and to imagine a baby that small being operated on was a daunting experience. However, her little personality had already revealed she was a feisty little girl. She would fight the ventilator and rear her little head back, trying to communicate *her* needs to the world. Knowing that, I knew she could pull through a surgery like a champ. The neonatologist explained that it would involve placing a small titanium clip on the artery to get it to close. He had performed the surgery many times and was confident that it would be successful. It was. She was in recovery mode for several days after the surgery, but then the most wonderful thing happened. The doctors cleared her for what they called "swaddle time".

In swaddle time, the nurses wrap the baby in blankets and allow you to hold her on your chest. I could *finally* hold her! The day came for the swaddle time and the nurses removed as many of the lines as they could, and they placed her on my bare chest. I sang softly in her ear and my husband came close. She looked at me and looked at him in response to our voices as we spoke. Kendra knew we were her parents and we loved her. Even though a month had gone by before we could hold her, the love and connection was never lost.

We believed the worst was over and her recovery would be clear sailing from here. However, surgery reared its ugly head *again*. This time, we were out with friends and returning to the hospital on the train when the doctors called. They needed to see us *immediately* to discuss a problem in her digestive system. When we arrived at the hospital, the doctor explained that Kendra had developed a condition called necrotizing enterocolitis, also called NEC. It is an inflammatory condition that usually occurs in premature babies. In her case, it had damaged parts of her small intestines leaving sections that were dead. The doctor explained, in surgery they could clip out the deadened areas and sew the remaining areas back together to create a shortened small bowel. We wondered how she would eat long term. How would she process food normally? The doctor reassured us based on a diagram he drew that she would have more than enough surface area of the intestines remaining to function normally. We were calmed by his reassurance.

Time was of the essence and we had to decide quickly because she was actively failing. The surgery went forward in response to the urgency. Once again, our feisty little Kendra came through like a champ. In fact, less than two weeks later, she was off the ventilator and breathing with regular oxygen by nasal cannula. Kendra improved so significantly, she no longer needed NICU level care. She was transferred to a step down unit for further recovery and weaning from tube feeding. All the work keeping my milk going paid off when she latched on the first time. I was clumsy getting her into proper "football" hold, but she latched on like she had been breastfeeding from day one. That's my girl, doing what comes naturally!

When the day came for discharge, she weighed five pounds eight ounces, and was off all monitors and oxygen. She was nursing for all her nutrition and growing normally. Our precious baby girl came home and our dream was fulfilled.

To look at her today, at almost twenty years old, with no health challenges, this all seems like a distant memory. We give glory to God for his faithfulness in preserving her life. For my husband and I, every tear and every prayer was well worth it.

Heather Harris dedicated 21 years of her career working as a physical therapist facilitating recovery mindsets in patients who were seeking to improve their health during challenging experiences. Use of these skills hit home when her daughter, Kendra, was born almost four months prematurely. That miraculous story of survival is shared in this book. Several years ago, Heather began a career transition as a certified coach with the John Maxwell Team helping others discover their deepest truth and operate in ways they never imagined they could. In the midst of this career shift, she has battled five years of her own health challenges. Heather has had to overcome complications from an autoimmune condition, stroke, skull surgery and speech impairment. She is no stranger to difficult circumstances, but has learned first-hand how to battle them and win.

Chapter 10
DAPO

My Conversion Story

I was born into a Muslim family in Lagos. Nigeria. Until I went to elementary school, I did not know any other religion besides Islam. When it was time to start elementary school, my parents enrolled me in a Baptist school in my neighborhood and that is where I first learned about the Christian faith. My teachers were all members of the Baptist church and they taught us the Bible with great passion. We were taught Bible stories and we sang hymns from, "Songs of Praise". I enjoyed singing those songs and I still sing some of them from memory today.

The goal of sending me to a Baptist school was not for me to become a Christian, but to ensure that I had a very good education. The Baptist school was one of the best.at the time. However, I did not realize until later in life that it was during my time in elementary school that the seed of the Christian Faith was being sown into my life. My parents had done their best to raise me in the way of Islam, and to this end, they sent me to an Islamic school on the weekends to learn the Quran. I did learn what I could and was a Muslim for many years.

After elementary school, I proceeded to secondary school (high school) and eventually to the university. In my final year in university, I started to feel an emptiness that I did not understand. I started to seek God more. I did not miss my five daily prayers as a Muslim, but that feeling of emptiness persisted. I graduated from the university with a bachelor's degree in Linguistics. Even though I graduated with honors, that feeling of emptiness was still there. I proceeded to complete my national year of service, a mandatory service to my country, but in all that time, the feeling of emptiness never left.

When my year of national service was over, the option was to either get a job or go back to school. I chose to go back to school. This time I chose to go to Law school. During my first year in Law school, I visited my sister in Medical school for her 21st birthday. That is where the story of my life changed. My sister, who had herself become a Christian, had a praise party to celebrate her birthday and I was invited to be a part of it. That was not the first time I was attended a Christian fellowship, so I knew some of the songs and to be honest I had a great time at the praise party. The leader of the fellowship prayed for me and that was the last thing I remember until I came round and found myself on the floor. I asked my sister what had happened, and she told me that I had been slain in the spirit. Whilst I did not understand what that meant then, I later understood it after I became a Christian.

When the praise party ended, my sister and I went back to her dormitory and she had me sleep in her bed. Little did I know that was a special night as I had a visitation from an angelic being. The area surrounding the bed I slept in was lit up so bright that it was blinding. My visitor who wore pure white, sat across from me and spoke with me through the night. When I woke up in the morning I felt as though a huge burden had been lifted off me and that feeling of emptiness was not as intense as it was the previous day.

I went back to my Law school without sharing my experience with anyone. I started to attend a Christian fellowship with my friends, and it was always such a joy. The songs were uplifting and Bible study was refreshing. Although the feeling of emptiness was no longer as intense as it used to be, it had not completely left me. One day, a friend gave me a tape of Jimmy Swaggart's sermon. At the end, he gave an invitation to receive Christ while singing, "Just as I am without one plea…" I knelt down in my dorm room and invited Jesus into my heart. That day, the feeling of emptiness left as suddenly had it had come, and I knew that my life was different.

Now that I had received Christ, I was filled with joy and I shared with my Christian friends who boldly encouraged me and prayed with me. I started attending a Bible-believing church but did not tell my parents because I knew I would face a tough time with them. I prayed fervently for grace to hold on to the end and God sent me friends to pray with me and encourage me in preparation for when I would go home. When it was time to go home at the end of the semester, I had been grounded enough in the word of God and prayer to decide that I would continue to follow Jesus and face whatever was dealt to me by my parents. I had stumbled on, "I Dared to Call Him Father" by Bilquis Sheikh. She was a Muslim woman who had survived persecution from her Muslim family, and I was encouraged to hold on to Jesus, the author and finisher of my faith.

My parents eventually found out that I had received Jesus Christ as my savior and they were both very displeased to say the least. My father was ready to disown me and I was ready to be disowned. I knew that if my parents rejected me, the Lord would receive me and take care of me. I remember the day my late mom threatened to beat me until I renounced Christ and I ran out of the house barefoot. I must have walked at least six miles to get to the house of a friend, but I was determined to hold on especially in view of the divine visitation during my sister's birthday. Somehow, I knew that Jesus was real and I was not going to let him go. For several weeks, I was unable to go back home because I did not know what to expect of my parents. During that time, my sisters in Christ walked the journey with me. I had left home with just the clothes on my back and my brethren at the law school, both male and female, made sure that I did not lack any good thing.

I am especially grateful to one of them who I will call Sister Reni. She took me into her home and gave me a room in her family's boys quarters. It was a difficult time, but the Lord was with me and He brought me through. Sister Reni and I have remained friends since then. Although we started as Christian sisters, we are more like blood sisters many years later. She did get married to a Christian man and was blessed with children in her marriage. Her faithfulness to the Lord in caring for me was greatly rewarded in many ways which cannot be mentioned in this chapter.

I don't remember how long I was away from home for but after a while my mom's heart became tender and she started to look for me. She had no idea where I was and reached out to her adopted mom, our adopted grandmother, for help in finding me. Up until that time, our grandma had no idea what was going on and she immediately reached out to her contacts at the law school to find me and tell me to come and see her. When I went to see her, she was very compassionate, being herself a Christian. She promised to speak to my parents about my faith. God did use her to speak to my parents and they agreed to let me return home and be a Christian. That was a miracle and the result of much prayer from the brethren.

My boyfriend at the time I gave my life to Christ did not buy into the idea of me being born again. He thought I was losing it. The option was to marry him and give up my faith or end the relationship and keep my faith. It was not a hard decision for me. Rather than continue with the relationship and be forced to relinquish my faith, I chose to walk away and be married to Jesus. My thought at the time was that it was better to be single and saved than be married and heading to hell. It seemed a foolish thing to do at the time, especially seeing that a number of my friends were getting married but my love for Jesus was greater than my love for a man and I was content with being single. God was faithful and He kept me in the faith until two years later when I met a Christian man who I ended up getting married to. God is faithful and when we hold on to Him. He does not fail us.

Having known the peace that comes with knowing Jesus, I started to believe God for my friends and family members who had not yet been saved by Jesus. One after the other, they came to the saving knowledge of our Lord Jesus Christ. Many of my family members also came to know Jesus and it was a beautiful thing to be able to connect with my family and friends again but now on a different platform. It was great to be able to speak the same language with them as members of the same family – the family of Christ.

My grandma (whom God had used to bring me back to my parents) and I had many instances of sharing the word of God together and it was a joy to learn from her wealth of knowledge. She passed away still in the faith a few years after I returned home. She left me a legacy of faith in Jesus Christ to follow. My mom passed away almost ten years ago and I am grateful to God that she received Jesus as her savior before she passed into glory. Hallelujah to the Lord!

God has blessed me with different women in my life who have encouraged me to go on in the face of adversity. Had it not been for them, I don't know if I would be sharing my story today. To the women who held my crown and prevented it from falling, even when I thought it would, I am eternally grateful and my goal in life is to pay it forward. That is why I am constantly encouraging women through my podcasts and YouTube channel to walk in the Empowerment that God has given them and not be afraid.

Beloved sister reading this, I can assure you that fear will try to hold you back, but you must arise boldly and reach out to other women who can hold your crown so that it does not fall off your head.

Dapo Lipede is a certified leadership coach and speaker with the John Maxwell Team. She is a seasoned teacher of the Bible and, both she and her husband pastor The Redeemed Christian Church of God, Living Faith Sanctuary in Colorado Springs. Dapo was born and raised a Muslim but an encounter with Jesus Christ in 1985 changed her life for good. She has since had the privilege of ministering Christ to others in her sphere of influence and bringing them to Jesus through her testimony. Dapo is the author of "Thinking Out Loud" books volumes 1 & 2 and she is currently working on Volume 3 which she expects to be published by the end of 2021. Dapo is the host of "The Empowered Woman Channel" on YouTube and she is passionate about Empowering Women so that they can live their lives to the fullest and raise godly children (where applicable) who will honor the Lord.

CHAPTER 11
JACQUELINE

#GIRLPOWER

Since childhood, I dreamt of marrying a handsome man with light eyes and hair. I wanted one daughter, one son and a white picket fence in the suburbs of Chicago. Sounds pretty stereotypical for a farmer girl that grew up with her grandparents. I have worked for 30 years to make this dream come true. In high school, I was in a horrific car accident that ended my athletic future; a path I had been on my entire life. I worked hard to rehabilitate myself back into high school. Even though I had lost my entire identity after that car accident, I kept my other dream alive. I met a boy who I fell for. He didn't have light eyes and hair, but I thought to myself, oh well, he is fabulous. I will alter my dream because I want him.

As a couple, we fought many societal battles because we were an interracial couple. It only strengthened our love. After college, we married and had two daughters. I wasn't blessed with a son and

I didn't continue trying. I figured God knew better. I still got to keep my dream of being married to a handsome man and having two children. I did it! I completed the American dream by twenty-five! What more could I want in life?

In my twenties, I may have appeared to have it all but on the inside, I was dead. I had low self-esteem which caused me to overcompensate by being a loud extravert who caused trouble for attention. I had a lot of unhealthy coping mechanisms such as drugs and alcohol that didn't fall in line with my morals and values. I loved that I accomplished what most people couldn't or didn't but it didn't change my inside feelings. Nothing changed them until he left me. My high school sweetheart, my husband, the father of my children, my best friend left me on my grandmothers' farm to care for her with dementia. I was finishing my master's degree with my daughters that were five and seven as well as his niece who was twelve. My unhealthy coping mechanisms took over my free time and became quite destructive. I was lost. I was hurting. I wasn't me. I wanted to feel something other than pain and shame. I wanted to be good enough. I wanted to be good enough for him. I wanted to be good enough for them. This entire time I worried about everyone else except me. I should have wanted to be good enough for ME!

Jesus took the wheel when I was spiraling, and no one could grab hold of me. I was in another car accident. This time, it was completely my fault. I almost ended up in a river. God spared my life once again. The morning after I was arrested, I remember my mom saying to me, "Are you ready to do something different with your life?" At that point, I got clean. I got rid of EVERYTHING: alcohol, drugs, bad foods, bad habits and even bad friends. I started taking vitamins and not just any vitamins.

I learned my chemical make-up and what my brain was lacking. This solved my self-esteem issues along with removing addiction. This was the hardest and most rewarding thing I had ever done in my life. I rebuilt myself by the grace of God and reclaimed who I was...a child of God. People didn't believe it and people didn't want to associate with me. I became boring. I was lost in society when I found myself in Christ. I just wanted to be good enough. This time for God.

This wasn't the dream I had for decades. It was a nightmare that I couldn't seem to fully crawl out of until I started getting to really know God. I started loving myself more. I bought a house for just me and my girls. I changed careers and leaped outside of my comfort zone. At that moment, I started living. I was no longer surviving. Then I met a man with light hair and eyes who had two sons. I fell for this man. We thought we could have it all in life. Together, after struggling in our own lives to find peace and happiness. Having a blended family is definitely not for the faint at heart. It took years to find happiness and peace through the chaos.

By thirty-five, I had it all again. The husband with light eyes and hair, two daughters, two step-sons, and I finally got my white picket fence. This husband wanted me to have my dreams come true. He built the fence for me to see as I looked out of my office window. I was in heaven. I survived trauma and still got my life back.

I never felt resilient through any of the situations I got myself into along the way. It was comfortable to me. It was how my life always functioned. I lived a life where I thrived in chaos. It was hard to not feel like an idiot for the decisions I had made in the past. It's hard to not dwell on the things I am ashamed of people knowing. I am a smart independent woman raised by a smart independent woman. How could I allow myself to be so foolish? Being raised Italian catholic taught me to not cry about life. For the record, that is not healthy. Many of us come from families with unhealthy characteristics that we keep passing on from generation to generation. Any time something happened, it was, "What are you crying for?" The world keeps turning. I barely ever cried throughout my life. I was taught it was weak to grieve. Think about how many people were raised similar to me. How many people in this world are unable to express emotions in a healthy light because of these horrific stereotypes?

During the global pandemic, new darkness came to light. I learned my handsome husband that spoiled me like crazy and loved me so much was a narcissist. I had no idea until someone told me. Then, the little MBA forever learner in me had tunnel vision on learning everything about narcissist. WOW oh WOW. What have I gotten myself into this time? How could I have been so blind? If this is not love, what is love? I realized at that moment that I was being abused for years and I thought it was love. How did that happen? I had been controlled, manipulated and love-bombed for years.

Did you know a true narcissist will never let you go? Oh boy, this was quite a challenge I had on my hands to escape. As I was creating my escape plan and getting my army together to help me, many people asked me one question, "How do you know he is?" He didn't care about my needs anymore. My body was rejecting him for years. I couldn't fathom being intimate with him. I just performed my wifely duty that he demanded. I was throwing up every day. My teeth began to decay from the stress of trying to please him. I would take baths almost daily to avoid confrontation. I was dying inside and felt like a prisoner. Everything I worked for meant nothing at that point. I had to go into fight or flight mode. I had no more fight in me especially during a global pandemic.

My reality, my truth was no longer mine. He had full control and not my best interests at heart. Once my eyes were open and I started to stand up for myself, things went downhill quickly. Between the mental, emotional and physical abuse, I couldn't think straight. We were stuck in the house 24/7. I couldn't escape it...until I escaped it. I packed a suitcase and a bookbag along with my daughters who were allowed to pack the same. We drove across the country to reclaim our life. I worked so hard to acquire the half-million-dollar home and the Mercedes along with the truck and motorcycle for him. We had it all, but we really had nothing because we no longer had each other. I have learned so much about myself on this journey. I stopped worrying about my five-year-old self dream. I learned, if I allow people to love me, they are inspired by me, loyal to me and help me. When he stopped doing all those things, I was DONE. I convinced him to file for a divorce. When he filed, I put my plan into action. The funniest thing is that it wasn't my plan at all. It was God's plan that he had been telling me about for six months. It was time to run and reclaim the life God intended me to have. Not the one I was insistent upon having. WOW...WOW...WOW, it was so clear.

My army rose together and helped carry me through. I wasn't resilient because of me. I am resilient because of him. God has carried me through every battle I have fought. Sometimes, it's not my way. Sometimes, it doesn't make sense initially. However, all the time, he loves me and waits for me to ask for his help. He is why I am resilient. Listen closely. Watch who he puts in your life. I truly believe everyone is a reason, season or a lifetime. Let the cards fall as they may. Our job is to put our armor of God on every day and seize the day. Live in light and truth. If we all woke up every day, prayed, put our armor on, seized the day and lived in light and truth, wouldn't we all become resilient human beings?

Jacqueline Proffit, a Chicago native, has walked through the fire many times in her life. Her faith in God's guidance has pulled her through every time. She believes in breaking down society's stereotypes and protecting God's child in every way she can. As a mother of two daughters, she is passionate about rehabilitating children rescued from sex trafficking through Sarah's Home. As the Financial Unicorn, she gives back to her community by counseling business owners and families on healing traumas surrounding behaviors related money. She hopes to bring peace and strength to other women that have been through similar situations. #GIRLPOWER

CHAPTER 12
MICHELLE

*"If you put a small value on yourself, rest
assured the world will not raise your price.
Pay no attention to what the critics say.
A statue has never been erected in honor
of a critic."*
– Jean Sibelius

My life wasn't always rainbows and butterflies. I went from "baby of the family" to the eldest sister. We've all been teenagers and had to survive through our insecurities. Unfortunately, some experiences are more crippling to self-esteem than others.

My childhood was spent as a military "brat" overseas in my mother's country of birth, the Philippines. I am the fourth child of six children. I have three older siblings, a six-year gap to me, then a 10-year gap to the twins. Our family got along well. We kids spent quality time together and generally enjoyed each other.

That said, we were always being compared. Not as a negative, rather, it's how we were identified.

The eldest brother was praised for being a talented musician. The next eldest brother was praised for his athletic abilities. The third, my elder sister, was praised for her natural grace and beauty. Then, there was me. I was okay at what the other three were great at, but not stellar. The youngest twins were too little to be part of the equation at the time. My siblings were being introduced to a house guest with each of their attributes being highlighted. When my father got to me, he said, "… and this is Michelle. She's smart". No animated descriptor. What did my 12-year-old mind create as a story? My mind developed the narrative that I had no talent in music, I was not athletic and I was not beautiful. Sure, I was "smart" but, that wasn't as exciting as the other descriptions used on my siblings.

One thought that stood out to me is the notion that a person needed more than being smart to succeed since, "the world opens for beautiful people". My mind completed the phrase with, "… like my sister". I created an entire foundation of insecurities based on my comparisons to my older siblings. Please note, these comparisons were not meant to hurt anyone. They were truthful observations. The comments weren't meant to degrade one over the other. Somehow, my mind created a story that if those attributes described my siblings, they were not meant for me. Think back to your childhood. Did you do the same? Did you interpret a compliment for another as a detriment to yourself?

In my late teens, as typical, I compared myself to my peers and to the women I saw in movies, television and even toys. It was my custom to watch who was considered beautiful, popular, and what was trending. This was a strange and confusing time for me. I was a teen in the 1980s. Big hair, feathered bangs, being blonde and leggy was the trend. I had the big Chaka Khan hair. That was as close to the popular image I achieved. The popular dolls were blonde bombshells of which were unachievable for a short, French-Creole/Filipina. Would there be no reprieve from my shortcomings?

I recorded each of my observations within my heart and mind. I created such a formative negative self-actualization playlist that I kept on repeat. I believed it. What I discovered is self-esteem issues grow like a cancer inside our souls. Especially when the initial criticism comes from someone you love, trust and respect. These negative seeds can be planted by siblings, parents, teachers, coaches, relatives, friends without their knowledge, and yourself. These are the most destructive. The feelings deep in my psyche prevented me from trying, and at times lead me to stay in negative relationships.

When I was in college full-time, I was on my own and working several jobs. While at my weekend job at a restaurant, the other servers asked if we could have a small gathering at my studio apartment. We were all the same age, but I was the only one who didn't live with my parents. I agreed with the caveat that everyone must leave by one AM because I had to sleep before I needed to drive to my other job. After our shift at the restaurant was over, we met at my apartment to play board games and unwind.

We were all having a good time when one of the servers said he had invited the new boy to join us. He was from out of town and didn't know many people. There was a knock at the door and the new boy enters. He seemed nice enough. We all had a good time together until one AM when everyone left as planned. I got ready for bed and had the small 20-inch television on. I hadn't unfolded my sofa-bed out to retire for the evening, when there was knock at the door. I looked out the peep hole and saw the new boy at my door.

Me: "Everyone is gone."

Him: "I forgot my jacket in your closet."

I looked in the closet and didn't see a jacket.

Me: "There isn't a jacket."

Him: "I put it on the shelf."

I stepped away from the closet and sure enough, well out of my reach was a black leather jacket.

I was far too short to reach the jacket and I didn't have a chair to retrieve it, so I opened the door. He strolled in, got his jacket and jumped over the back of my sofa bed and sat to watch television.

Me: "You need to leave."

Him: "What would you say if you saw me on television?" (A police show was on.)

Me: "I'd act like I didn't see you."

Him: "Damn straight you would."

He proceeded to pull a gun from his jacket, pointed it at me and ordered me to sit next to him. He moved in and kept me as his captive victim for over 10 months. In public, he was the life of the party and everyone kept telling me I was so lucky to have someone who loved me. In private, he was a monster. All my self-doubt had me wondering if this was the only love I was worthy of. Even when I called the police, they said this was just a lover's quarrel and refused to get involved. I believed my life and the lives of everyone who knew me, were in danger. He threatened if I ever told what he was doing, he would slaughter whomever I told, while I was forced to watch. It would be my fault.

I share this tiny bit of my story because while I was repeatedly attacked by this boy, all my insecurities, my inner-critics and every negative comment I ever allowed into my mind boiled back up as confirmation of why he was doing what he was. I distinctly remember thinking during one of the earlier attacks that per-haps this is what I deserved. My instincts said, "Heck, no!" My mind rationalized that to keep everyone else safe, I should shut up. One afternoon after an exceptionally brutal attack, I begged to God, "What can I do?" I literally received a response from a booming voice that came from all around me, "You're smarter than him." The compliment I received as a child that I thought was a curse, was my blessing. I devised a plan to safely escape his control. It worked. He never followed through on his threats to eliminate my family and friends. I survived.

Many years later, I got married, had children, travelled the world and seemed as if I had my life under control. I played small. Whenever I would start to succeed, I would sabotage it. I had to stay hidden for fear he would find me again. My life was an illusion. It took me years and intentional steps toward love, acceptance and self-actualization to realize I was still under the spell of my crushed self-esteem.

You may think that things said when you were a child were so long ago – get over it! The reality is, the level of self-esteem a teen has can set the stage for their entire life. Think upon your own insecurities or the insecurities of someone you care for.

"I can't talk in front of all those people – they'll laugh at me."

"Don't take my picture – I'm ugly!"

"I'm going to have plastic surgery (my eyes are too far apart; my nose too big, etc.)"

"I'm so stupid!"

"I'm sorry…I can't…"

"I don't deserve a person who will treat me with respect."

Words are powerful. Be careful how you use them and how you perceive them.

Throughout my youth, I heard simple words from various individuals. Inadvertently, I gathered these together to define who I believed I was. I took each statement and word to create a mountain of bricks in which I built my fortress of safety. Why would anyone choose to place themselves in a prison of negativity? Perhaps it was a comfort zone for myself where I could live my life from a point of lack. I can't fail if I am not worthy of anything.

According to the National Report on the State of Self-Esteem, commissioned by the Dove® Self-Esteem Fund, the words and actions of parents play a pivotal role of fostering positive self-esteem in girls. Those with low self-esteem are less likely to receive praise from either parent and more likely to receive criticism than girls with high self-esteem. A girl's self-esteem is more strongly related to how she views her own body shape and weight, than how much she actually weighs.

Many individuals do not recognize they have self-esteem issues. Many don't realize that the self-esteem issues that began in our teen years have followed us into adulthood. What I ask of you today, is to look into yourself. Examine what is holding you back from your dreams. If you discover it to be something you were told as a child…, is it really defining you now? Be who YOU are, not what others believe you to be. Just because an individual or situation has brought you to the brink of crushing your spirit, mind or will – it doesn't define who you CHOOSE to be. It is up to us whether we choose to learn from the experience or let the experience define us. Take off the discount tag. We are priceless!

Here are three lessons to incorporate into your life:

1. **Love yourself**
    This is a necessity! Without self-love none of the other steps will work. You must value yourself so highly, that no person or situation can pull you into despair. You need to love yourself beyond the perceptions of everyone around you. You are special and deserve complete love and adoration. You are the queen of your life! Wear your preverbal, or literal, crown proudly.

2. **Remove negativity from your life (even if they are family)**
You've heard the saying, "one bad apple ruins the barrel". The concept works with your environment. The people in your life directly or indirectly influence your thoughts. As the queen of your life, it is imperative to control whom you allow to be your advisors. Nothing would be accomplished if all you have in your life are people who focus on negativity or don't support your aspirations. Yes, it will probably be difficult but think of all the growth you can experience without someone dragging you back. Let them go.

3. **Surround yourself with love and support**
Throughout the stories in this book, you heard of the importance of having a tribe. What do we mean? A tribe is a group of people you choose to be closer than family. They share your hopes, dreams, aspirations and you know you will not be demeaned or judged. A tribe will provide you honest feedback without leaving you deflated. They are inspired, passionate, motivated, grateful and open-mined. Your tribe will never use or take advantage of you. They are the wind you need to soar and will keep your flame roaring strong enough to fuel you to your next endeavor. Most of all, your tribe allows you to be unapologetically you! They are the love and support foundation that you know will be ready to hold your crown when you need to take it off for a bit. Your tribe will set your crown back upon your head when you forget to put it back on. Bottom line: Your tribe defines your vibe – they are the reflection of who you are and strive to be.

Together, we can break the cycle of abuses to self and others. The women in this book have shown that it can be done! Despite all hardships these women had to endure, they are all happy and successful today. We need to break the chains of family norms, societal expectations and crossing through generational stigmas. Everyone is special in their own way. As we hope our stories connected with you, share your stories within your families, communities and beyond. The more we share what we have endured and survived, the more hope we give to others experiencing trials. By being brave, you show others that there is something better yet to come and it is acceptable to share their stories.

Pick up your crown.
Dust if off.
Wear it with pride.

Michelle Mras is a survivor of multiple life challenges to include a Traumatic Brain Injury and Breast Cancer. She guides others to recognize the innate gifts within them, stop apologizing for what they are not and step into who they truly are… Unapologetically.

She accomplishes this through one-on-one and group coaching, Training events, Keynote talks, her books, and Podcasts.

Michelle has been awarded the Inspirational Women of Excellence Award from the Women Economic Forum, New Delhi, India; the John Maxwell Team Culture Award for Positive Attitude; Winner of the Ultimate Speaker Competition and has speaking parts in a few Sci-Fi movies check the IMDB.com database for her; has been featured on hundreds of Podcasts, radio programs, several magazines, quoted in books and has a habit of breaking out into song.

Michelle's driving thought is that every day is a gift. Tomorrow is never promised. Every moment is an opportunity to be the best version of you… Unapologetically!

More Books From

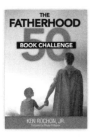

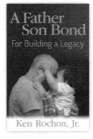

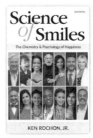

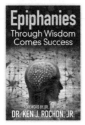

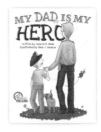

www.PerfectPublishing.com